Muhammad Reconsidered

MUHAMMAD RECONSIDERED

A Christian Perspective on Islamic Prophecy

ANNA BONTA MORELAND

University of Notre Dame Press
Notre Dame, Indiana

University of Notre Dame Press
Notre Dame, Indiana 46556
undpress.nd.edu

Copyright © 2020 by the University of Notre Dame

Published in the United States of America

Library of Congress Cataloging-in-Publication Data

Names: Moreland, Anna Bonta, author.
Title: Muhammad reconsidered : a Christian perspective
on Islamic prophecy / Anna Bonta Moreland.
Description: Notre Dame : University of Notre Dame Press, [2020] |
Includes bibliographical references and index.
Identifiers: LCCN 2019054886 (print) | LCCN 2019054887 (ebook) |
ISBN 9780268107253 (hardback) | ISBN 9780268107284 (adobe pdf) |
ISBN 9780268107277 (epub)
Subjects: LCSH: Prophecy—Christianity. | Prophecy—Islam. |
Thomas, Aquinas, Saint, 1225?–1274. |
Muhammad, Prophet, –632—Prophetic office. |
Christianity and other religions—Islam. | Islam—Rellations—Christianity.
Classification: LCC BR115. P8 M64 2020 (print) |
LCC BR115. P8 (ebook) | DDC 261.2/7—dc23
LC record available at https://lccn.loc.gov/2019054886
LC ebook record available at https://lccn.loc.gov/2019054887

In memoriam
Michael J. Buckley, S.J.

Say: "People of the Book! Come now to a word common between us and you, that we serve none but God, and that we associate not aught with Him, and do not some of us take others as Lords, apart from God."

—Qur'an 3:64

[Muslims] professing to hold the faith of Abraham, along with us adore the one and merciful God, who on the last day will judge humankind.

—*Lumen Gentium* 16

CONTENTS

ACKNOWLEDGMENTS

This book emerged out of the experience of teaching an upper-level theology course at Villanova University titled "Judaism, Christianity and Islam in Dialogue." My department allowed me to teach a course outside my area of expertise through which I learned a tremendous amount. I began to think and write in the area of the theology of religious pluralism because of questions posed by students over the years in that class. I am grateful to each of these cohorts for encouraging me to think more deeply about the relationship between Christianity and Islam.

Initial ideas for this book project were published in two articles: "Analogical Reasoning and Christian Prophecy: The Case of Muhammad," in *Modern Theology* 29, no. 4 (October 2013) and "The Qur'an and the Doctrine of Private Revelation: A Theological Proposal," in *Theological Studies* 76, no. 3 (September 2015). The bulk of this book was written during my time as the Myser Visiting Fellow (2015–2017) at the University of Notre Dame's de Nicola Center for Ethics and Culture. The director of the center, Carter Snead, offered extraordinary support during my research leave, not least of which was employing my research assistant, Mariele Courtois, whose meticulous work improved my overall argument. Villanova University granted me a sabbatical year and then a research leave to work on this book manuscript. During my time at the University of Notre Dame, Gabriel Said Reynolds graciously agreed to allow me to sit in on his doctoral seminar on Muhammad, and Jean Porter generously invited me to talk about my book project with the Department of Theology's doctoral students.

While too many colleagues to enumerate have helped in the development of this book, I have to single out the members of the Aquinas Studium, the John Carroll/Catholic University of America (CUA)

Muslim-Catholic Dialogue, and the faculty in the Villanova Department of Humanities. Every summer for about a decade, I have met with colleagues from the United States and Canada to read Aquinas together for a weeklong seminar. During one summer (2014), we read Aquinas on prophecy to help me test out the argument of this book. The members of the John Carroll/CUA Muslim-Catholic Dialogue discussed two chapters of my manuscript in March 2018, and the members of the Department of Humanities at Villanova University read drafts of my first and last chapters in May 2018. I am grateful for comments and questions from those I met workshopping the book's central argument at the Newman Institute University College in Uppsala, Sweden, Marquette University, and La Universidad Católica de Argentina in Buenos Aires. Jeremy Wilkins and Grant Kaplan each read parts of my manuscript, and I owe a special debt of gratitude to Rita George-Tvrtkovic and Alasdair MacIntyre for having the patience to read and comment on the entire manuscript. At different stages in the writing process, the enthusiasm and support of Peter Ochs, Alasdair MacIntyre, and Gavin D'Costa were invaluable.

I would like to thank Villanova University's Subvention of Publication program for supporting the publication of the image on the cover of this book. The image is part of an illustrated manuscript of Mustafā Darīr's *Siyar-i-Nabī* [The Life of the Prophet] from the Ottoman era (1594–95). It is the largest sixteenth-century manuscript produced during the reign of Murād III. The image depicts the archangel Gabriel handing the prophet Muhammad the Qur'an. My book can be read as a meditation on this image.

I dedicate this book to my dissertation director and mentor, the late Michael J. Buckley, S.J., not because he had any direct influence on its development but rather because, without the care and training he gave me so many years ago, I would not have had the discipline to tighten the argument through endless drafts. His is the voice in my head that is rarely satisfied. I owe him an enormous debt of gratitude.

I know of no other editor who is as insightful, helpful, and patient as Stephen Wrinn of the University of Notre Dame Press. Working with him has been a privilege. I also would like to thank the three anonymous readers of my manuscript and copyeditor Marilyn Martin, who provided comments to improve the final manuscript, and the work-study students in the Villanova Department of Humanities, who helped compile the bibliography and did other fact-checking work.

Finally, my husband, Michael, has been a true companion to me in all things, but particularly as I shepherded this book to its completion. Our four children—Juan Pablo, Sebastian, Margarita, and Tomas—have had no other choice than to be patient with their mother and her laptop.

CHAPTER ONE

Setting the Stage

It has been twenty years since Samuel Huntington set forth his controversial argument about the fundamental incompatibility between Islamic cultures and Western cultures influenced by Christianity.[1] Apart from the wider contested claims, he urged his readers to develop a deeper understanding of the basic religious assumptions underlying other civilizations.[2] Twenty-five years later, the need to understand non-Western religious traditions has become all the more pressing.

THE GLOBAL CONTEXT

While Huntington's work has received sharp criticism in several academic circles,[3] his thesis has shaped debates during the past few decades about Muslim emergence in the West. Western assumptions about "religion," broadly speaking, color these encounters and ultimately hinder a fruitful dialogue among those from the secular West and those from Muslim majority countries. These assumptions come in two fundamental forms: "religion as universal norms" and "religion as extremism." Historically, the development of the first assumption directly led to the second. Both are dependent on a founding myth of the modern that invents the term "religion," either by paring it down to a meaningless lowest common denominator of universal norms for morality or by associating it with irrationality and violence. Neither of these modes of engagement provides a fruitful way of encountering actual religious traditions because the dimensions that are most crucial to particular religious communities—such as revelation, prophecy, sin, or righteousness—are either attacked as extremist or ignored as superstitious. This has particularly pernicious consequences for Western encounters with Muslim belief and practice.

Historically, the first assumption about religious belief that has emerged in modernity reduces religion to universal norms. Some would argue that Friedrich Schleiermacher is the quintessential modern religious thinker who, in trying to make religious belief palatable to his audience, robbed Christianity of its distinctiveness. In his *On Religion* (1799) he characterized religious belief as fundamentally a feeling of "absolute dependence" and then built a theology on this universal "religious self-consciousness" in *Christian Faith* (1821). In some readings, religion became a feature of human self-consciousness. Or one can look at Cleanthes' defense of religious belief in David Hume's *Dialogues Concerning Natural Religion* (1776) to find God as the explanatory principle of the world. Once universal norms were found through anthropology, physics, philosophy, or ethics, traditional religious belief became superfluous. Michael Buckley traces this narrative in his *At the Origins of Modern Atheism* (1987) and its sequel, *Denying and Disclosing God: The Ambiguous Project of Modern Atheism* (2004). Buckley argues that the move to make religion "rational" paradoxically led to an atheism that equates religion with irrationality and danger. It was exactly the feckless religion invented, for example, by the universal norms of Descartes (mathematics), Newton (mechanics), or Kant (ethics) that turned religion into something at first unnecessary and eventually antihuman. It was the effort to set religious belief on solid rational ground that resulted in its own undoing.

God became an unnecessary explanatory principle of the universe and, ultimately, a projection of human needs and fears. Ludwig Feuerbach portrayed religion as a projection of human desires in his *The Essence of Christianity* (1841) and urged his readers to cast off this infantile crutch. Sigmund Freud translated this insight into the psychological arena in his *The Future of an Illusion* (1927), while Karl Marx developed this insight in economics in his *Critique of Hegel's Philosophy of Right* (begun in 1843), as did Friedrich Nietzsche in philosophy in *The Gay Science* (1882). Reducing religious belief strictly to universal norms creates a certain tone deafness, making it impossible to understand what motivates and maintains many contemporary religious believers. Any attempt to understand religious traditions through this lens ignores the most fundamental aspects of religious belief. In Buckley's terms, this move brackets the religious.[4] Ironically, the attempt to make religion palatable to modern rationalists ultimately pushed religious belief into the realm of irrationality, a realm that endangered the modern political order.

Having now reached a point where religious belief is equated with extremism and violence, we will examine this assumption closely as it has become firmly embedded in Western consciousness and shapes encounters today with Muslims in particular. Muslims have been inserted smoothly into a fable about the death of religion in modernity. Modern Europeans who long thought that the religious commitments of old had finally subsided are finding themselves in a new situation. Schleiermacher's early nineteenth-century "cultured despisers of religion" appear tame when compared to Europeans two hundred years later, who believe that religious belief inevitably breeds fanaticism and violence. Many in the modern West assume that since Hobbes and Locke, Hume and Kant had entered the European intellectual bloodstream, the rest of the world would eventually follow suit and lay aside the violent passions of religion. Here is Mark Lilla in a 2007 *New York Times Magazine* article on the fanaticism of religious belief: "Though we have our own fundamentalists, we find it incomprehensible that theological ideas still stir up messianic passions, leaving societies in ruin. We had assumed this was no longer possible, that human beings had learned to separate religious questions from political ones, that fanaticism was dead. We were wrong."[5]

The terrorist attacks from 9/11 in New York to San Bernardino, from Paris to Brussels and elsewhere, have been conveniently folded into this narrative. Islamic extremists have no interest in Mark Lilla's "Great Separation" between politics and religion outlined in his 2007 *The Stillborn God*. The problem with the account from Lilla and others lies in their insistence on equating religious belief generally—whether Muslim, Christian, or otherwise—with superstition, irrationality, and extremism. Those who are convinced by this narrative equate religion with terrorism. We cannot let religiously committed Muslims from around the world or Christians from the global South challenge our assumptions about either the irrational fanaticism of religion or the attraction of its substitute, the global marketplace.[6]

Consider Mark Lilla's argument in *The Stillborn God* that before the wars of religion in the seventeenth century, humans generally had drawn on God when reflecting about political questions. In response to these wars, some European intellectuals moved away from "political theology." Lilla's book tells the story of this "great separation" in which, for children of Hobbes, "a decent political life could not be realized within the terms set by Christian political theology, which bred violent eschatological passions."[7] Religion, in Lilla's view, can "express dark fears and desires," it can "destroy community by dividing its members," and it can "inflame the mind with destructive apocalyptic fantasies of immediate redemption."[8] We in the West are heirs to this fragile separation, but we live among those whose politics are still inflamed by their theology. In a 2014 article in the *New Republic*, Lilla writes, "Outside the Islamic world, where theological principles still have authority [sic], there are fewer and fewer objections that persuade people who have no such principles."[9] If drawing on theological principles to answer political questions leads to apocalyptic fantasies, it's best to keep any theology out of the public square.[10]

William Cavanaugh's *The Myth of Religious Violence* (2009) and David Bentley Hart's *Atheist Delusions* (2010) show how this narrative has been a legitimating myth of Western societies. As the myth goes, since religions had posed regular threats to civil order before the Enlightenment, securing peace entailed separating church from state and relegating religious beliefs and passions to the private sphere. Modern political life requires an unbiased secular foundation. Cavanaugh argues that religious ideas are no more likely to set off violence than a whole host of "secular" ideas. The modern West, in fact, invents these categories and then uses the idea that "religion" is violent in order to justify the violence of "secular" orders. We in the West are thought of as reasonable and dispassionate, while Muslim religious fanatics are prone to violence: "*Their* violence is religious, and therefore irrational and divisive. *Our* violence, on the other hand, is secular, rational, and peacemaking. And so we find ourselves regrettably forced to bomb them into the higher rationality."[11] Hart observes that equating religion with violence ignores the fact that the modern secular age has been the most savagely brutal period of human history.[12] Both Cavanaugh and Hart trace the roots of this bloodshed to the birth of the nation-state in the emerging modern West.[13]

Learning to wean ourselves off of these assumptions about what constitutes religious belief and practice is the first step toward encountering Muslims with fresh ears. Religious traditions cannot be reduced to universal norms, as this move empties religious belief of its content in order to bring about a dangerously thin consensus—a consensus that many religious believers reject. But neither can they become reduced to irrational motivations for political action. Both assumptions about religious belief from those in the secular West—religion as universal norms[14] and religion as irrational—fail to lead to fruitful dialogue with religious believers in general and Muslims in particular.

A genuine understanding of religious traditions has become a theopolitical necessity in the West. While many secularists expected an inevitable decline of religious belief as Enlightenment modernity took hold around the globe, it seems that the exact opposite has occurred. As the authors of *God's Century: Resurgent Religion and Global Politics* wrote in 2009, "Over the past four decades, religion's influence on politics has reversed its decline and become more powerful on every continent and across every major world religion."[15] These authors argue that despite the prediction of the "secularization theory," the twenty-first century can ironically be coined "God's Century." In other words, religion has become and will likely continue to be a vital player in the global political realm. With regard to Islam in particular, Europe is now facing an influx of Muslim immigrants that does not fit this myth of the emergence and death of religion, does not subscribe to the seventeenth-century theists' understanding of religion, and rejects the religious/secular divide imposed by European colonialists. For many new residents of Western Europe, religion forms the central fabric of their lives. How will a post-Christian Europe absorb these new residents into their local communities? And how will it develop an understanding of

Islam that does not reduce it to modern universal principles applicable to anyone or equate it with extreme acts of violence?

Instead of shoehorning Islam into modern fabrications of "religion," fruitful dialogue could emerge if we read Muslim religious claims *through* Christian theological traditions rather than in spite of them. Pierre Manent persuasively argues in *Beyond Radical Secularism* (2016) that Europeans (in his case, his fellow French citizens) are ill prepared both to incorporate Muslims into their political community and to understand Islam. This is due not only to prejudices and widespread ignorance about Islam, even though plenty of both abound. This limitation also results from Europeans' having lost touch with their own Christian roots, whose *laïcité* vocabulary is ill equipped to engage Muslims in serious terms. Manent suggests toward the end of his book that the Catholic Church is poised to work as a mediator between the secular West and Islam: "Given the spiritual fragmentation that affects the Western world, [the Catholic Church] is the fixed point that is concerned to relate itself intelligently to all the other points and to which the other points can try to relate."[16]

An interpretation of Islam from within the Catholic tradition in particular offers an appreciation of one tradition from within the heart of another.[17] Catholic interpretations of Islam have been riddled, of course, with dangerous medieval caricatures and violent polemic that continue into the present.[18] Nevertheless, the Catholic tradition offers rich resources we can use to obtain a fresh understanding of Islam. The Catholic tradition offers intellectual resources and institutional networks to serve as mediator between Islam and the secular West since it has achieved a differentiation of the sacred from the secular that acknowledges the distinctiveness of the political realm without yielding to the thinness of the secular myth. It shares a guarded openness to the political liberalism of the West while remaining grounded in a religious worldview that is aligned in many ways with the Islamic tradition. Many Catholics still inhabit Charles Taylor's "enchanted world," despite living and working in modern cities and exhibiting many aspects of the "buffered self." The Church has been understood to be late in embracing the modern world. But, as Ulrich Lehner persuasively argues in his *The Catholic Enlightenment: The Forgotten History of a*

Global Movement (2016), "It was Catholicism that, at least during the first few decades of the eighteenth century, was able to interact productively with Enlightenment thought. Only the anti-clerical and anti-Christian attacks of Enlighteners—and especially the terror of the French Revolution—put a stop to this conversation."[19] To be sure, that engagement did not translate into an uncritical embrace of Enlightenment liberalism, but it did bear fruit in an openness to religious freedom and democratic forms of government during Vatican II. It is the argument of this book that the Catholic Church is particularly equipped to engage with Muslims in theological terms and that this will lead to salutary political consequences.

The Second Vatican Council (1962–65) is often understood as the Church's delayed embrace of modernity. For some, this embrace represents a fundamental break from the past. For others, it betrays centuries-old traditions and practices. Both, however, overdetermine the "embrace" that the Council represented. While it clearly updated certain elements of ecclesial thinking, it also engaged in a critical renewal of the theological tradition in ways that challenged the assumptions of modernity. It may be, for example, that the documents provide an opportunity for a new openness to Islam but in a way that recovers premodern resources deep within the Christian theological tradition. That is, in fact, the method used this book. The documents of the Second Vatican Council provide fertile ground for dialogue with Muslims, and yet they leave crucial questions unresolved. One of the two most important questions about Islam about which the Council chose to remain silent is the status of Muhammad among Catholics, especially given everything else the documents affirm about Islam. George Anawati, O.P., one of the visionaries behind the conciliar statements on Islam, commented on why the Council made no mention of Muhammad: "Obviously, this is the most sensitive point for the Moslems, and the Catholic experts have chosen to deal with it—by ignoring it. Once the dialogue is underway, this central point will have to be considered in more detail."[20] The Council's fresh understanding of Christian revelation provides the groundwork for a reappraisal of the prophet Muhammad in this book. But this reappraisal can happen only through a recovery of a medieval Christian account of prophecy. By marrying this account of prophecy to the groundbreaking claims from the Second Vatican Council about both Muslims and Christian revelation, in this book, I propose that Christians become open to the theoretical possibility that Muhammad is a religious prophet. In fact, this book prepares the theological groundwork for an examination of that possibility.

Let me clarify, however, what I do and do not mean by entertaining this question. I do not suggest that Muhammad was a Christian prophet who misunderstood his message. Nor do I suggest that Christians can adopt an Islamic theology of prophecy and accept the fundamental Islamic interpretation of Muhammad and his prophetic identity. Rather, with Thomas Aquinas, I will point to prophets in the Hebrew Scriptures who are drawn from "the nations," such as Job or Balaam, to argue for a Christian understanding of prophecy that reaches beyond the boundaries of the people of Israel and the Church.[21] Christians draw different messages from Hebrew prophets than Jews do, just as they draw different messages from Muhammad than Muslims do.[22] The Christian claim about Balaam's prophecy is both distinct and related to the Jewish claim; the argument of this book is that a similar pattern emerges between Christian and Islamic accounts of Muhammad's prophecy. In short, Christians have solid internal theological warrants for exploring the possibility that Muhammad was a religious prophet. What Christians mean by this will differ in fundamental ways from what Muslims proclaim in their profession of faith, or the Shahada ("There is no God but God, and Muhammad is his messenger"). But the Christian claim provides a new avenue to consider the invitation in *Nostra Aetate* (hereafter *NA*) to appreciate what is "true and holy" in Islam. At the same time, it provides a bridge of understanding and, importantly, a locus of good theological disagreement between Christians and Muslims, based upon a clarification of their different senses of prophecy. Such a disagreement, from a place of reverence, mutual understanding, and illumination, provides an alternative to the incommensurable "clash of civilizations" model without erasing the particular theological identities of either Christianity or Islam.

I hope that this book will reach at least three intended audiences: Christians who want to know what basis there is for extended and constructive conversation with Muslims, Muslims who are interested in contemporary Christian theological engagements with Islam, and those who are neither Christian nor Muslim but want to know how rival theological and moral traditions can enter into such conversation. The argument of this book is an exercise in Christian theology. In it I do not speak for Muslims, of course, but I do hope to address the critique made after Vatican II that the Church failed to engage the issue of the prophethood of Muhammad. It could be used in interreligious dialogue, but only as a secondary result of the primary work internal to the Christian tradition done here. Christians reading this book might already be raising an eyebrow, wondering how I can turn someone whom the medieval world deemed a dangerous heretic into a religious prophet. Some might ask whether I am a globalizing syncretist. Others might suggest that I am a colonizing traditionalist. Muslim readers might be wary that I am Christianizing their most revered founder and turning him into someone he is not. They might object that Muhammad can be a prophet for Christians only in Muslim terms.

Of these and other objectors I ask that they give this book a fair hearing. I argue here that deep within the bosom of one tradition (Christianity) one finds a theological openness to another, later tradition (Islam). And this means that Christians have internal reasons from within their tradition to take seriously the revelations Muhammad received in Mecca and Medina. In fact, Christians need to take all the resources used to interpret the Bible—historical, anthropological, philological, and theological—and apply them to a Christian reading of the Qur'an. Responding to *NA*'s call to appreciate the good and the true in Islam from within the Church's theological tradition will then serve as a model for others to engage Islam in deep theological terms. The political ramifications of these theological moves are wide-ranging, as they could reshape the Danes' understanding of the practice of circumcision, the Swiss consideration of girls who reject co-ed swimming instruction in schools, or the French injunctions against certain forms of female Muslim dress.[23] At the very least, it would encourage some to understand Muslims not as "religious others" but as related kin.

Addressing the question of the prophecy of Muhammad is not only a necessary political question; it is also a theological question that has not been sufficiently addressed in contemporary Catholicism. In fact, the documents from Vatican II, while offering the first boldly affirmative portrayals of Muslim belief and practice in magisterial texts *ever*, consciously left unresolved the question of the status of Muhammad as a prophet. We turn, then, to a brief sketch of this ecclesial history.

THE THEOLOGICAL CONTEXT

In March 2004, Rowan Williams, the former Archbishop of Canterbury, convened a group of thirty Muslim and Christian scholars to discuss the issue of prophecy. Daniel Madigan, an Australian Jesuit and professor at Georgetown University, observed during that seminar: "The question of Muhammad is without doubt the most avoided question in Muslim-Christian relations. One finds no mention of this Prophet of Islam, for example, in the otherwise laudatory comments made about Muslims and their faith in the groundbreaking documents of the Second Vatican Council. They give no sense at all that this faith has a founder and a history. And since that time the hesitancy about responding could hardly be said to have diminished."[24] The Roman Catholic Church has expanded, deepened, and clarified its teaching on other religions over the course of the past several decades.[25] But different factions in the Catholic Church have offered conflicting interpretations of the meaning of these teachings.[26] In addition, theologies of religious pluralism and comparative theologies blossomed after the Second Vatican Council. Among the most recent developments in these fields lies work comparing Christianity and Islam. While studies by theologians have begun to draw parallels between Jesus and the Qur'an (both of which became enfleshed) or Muhammad and Mary,[27] this book rises to Daniel Madigan's unspoken but implied challenge by investigating the status of Muhammad's prophecy. Muslims revere Jesus as a prophet. Does the Catholic understanding of prophecy allow for consideration of Muhammad as a prophet? Do reasons internal to the Catholic tradition warrant such a move?

This book addresses unresolved issues in the conciliar documents from Vatican II about the Church's stance toward Islam by applying a neglected aspect of Thomas's thought, his treatment of prophecy. This historical retrieval leads to a new understanding of Islam, one that honors the integrity of the Catholic tradition and, through that integrity, argues for the possibility in principle of Muhammad as a religious prophet.

OVERVIEW OF THE ARGUMENT

Important work from the past fifty years provides an understanding of the issues that gave rise to the Council, the heated debates that took place both inside and outside of the conciliar sessions, and the remaining issues that have developed in the postconciliar period. The contested question about whether Vatican II was an "event" that ruptured the Church's ties to the past or whether it was a "renewal within tradition" has planted ideological fault lines within the theological academy.[28] I argue in this book that one can interpret Vatican II with Benedict XVI's "hermeneutic of reform," where the Church's new attitude toward Islam first appeared discontinuous with the past. But further probing reveals that a medieval account of prophecy—freshly understood— already contains hidden seeds of Vatican II's claims about Islam. We can say, with Benedict XVI, "It is precisely in this combination of continuity and discontinuity at different levels that the very nature of true reform consists."[29] The creative question of the prophecy of Muhammad did not emerge at the magisterial level before the opening of the Council.[30] But a constructive answer to this question must be borne of a deep encounter with the Church's theological tradition.

Chapter 2 sets the stage for this inquiry through an intertextual reading of the key Vatican II documents. John O'Malley, S.J., suggests that while impressive research on the genesis, analysis, and redaction of the sixteen conciliar documents is already complete, we should now begin to interpret the lessons of the Council by reading each document as "in some measure an expression of larger orientations and as an integral part of a cohesive corpus, which is a result in large part of the documents' intertextual character."[31] Chapter 2 examines the Council's claims about Islam through the text of *Dei Verbum* (hereafter *DV*).

Discussions of the initial text of this constitution began in the opening days of the Council and continued during all of the sessions until its formal promulgation at the Council's close three years later. In many ways, the controversies concerning the articulation of the Church's understanding of revelation framed discussions of all the key conciliar documents. As a result, the radical reorienting of the Church's understanding of revelation in *DV* was substantively borne out in other conciliar documents in general and in the statements about other religions in particular.[32]

The concrete claims about Islam in *NA* and *Lumen Gentium* (hereafter *LG*) are read through the text of the theology of revelation found in *DV*. *DV* summarizes the conciliar reflections on the transmission and content of divine revelation. The Council moved away from an understanding of revelation as static propositions and toward a dynamic understanding of the unfolding of revelation in salvation history. This recognizes that "God who spoke of old still maintains an uninterrupted conversation with the bride of his beloved Son."[33] With respect to the concrete claims about Islam, *NA* affirms:

> They worship the one God living and subsistent, merciful and almighty, creator of heaven and earth, who has spoken to humanity and to whose decrees, even the hidden ones, they seek to submit themselves whole-heartedly, just as Abraham, to whom the Islamic faith readily relates itself, submitted to God. They venerate Jesus as a prophet, even though they do not acknowledge him as God, and they honour his virgin mother Mary and even sometimes devoutly call upon her. Furthermore they await the day of judgment when God will requite all people brought back to life. Hence they have regard for the moral life and worship God especially in prayer, almsgiving and fasting.[34]

LG is even more emphatic about the fact that Muslims and Christians honor the same God: "But the plan of salvation also embraces those who acknowledge the Creator, and among these the . . . [Muslims] are first; they profess to hold the faith of Abraham and *along with us* they worship the one merciful God who will judge humanity on the last day"[35] (emphasis mine). If, as *NA* suggests and *LG* explicitly affirms, Christians and Muslims honor the same God, and if, as the documents readily acknowledge, Christians and Muslims share an overlapping web of beliefs, we should not be surprised to find the Qur'an to be a vehicle of God's grace in Muslim communities. While *NA* does not mention the Qur'an or Muhammad, the Muslim beliefs that the document applauds did not appear in seventh-century Arabia without a messenger; they have not been preserved in Muslim religious life without being compiled in a sacred book. More importantly, however, if Muslims are listening to God speaking through the Qur'an, Christians should consider the possibility that acknowledging this experience could bring Christians to a deeper consideration of their own faith in God. Qur'anic passages heard and recorded by Muhammad, while not adding to the deposit of the faith, might enliven the faithful at a particular historical moment, helping them to more fully understand and live out the Gospel.

We will also examine ecclesial documents that emerged after the Council that pertain to our question. Central among these are *Dialogue and Proclamation (DP)* and *Guidelines for Dialogue between Christians and Muslims*, issued by the Pontifical Council for Inter-Religious Dialogue, *Redemptoris Missio (RM)*, promulgated by John Paul II, and *Dominus Iesus (DI)*, issued by the Congregation for the Doctrine of the Faith (CDF).[36] This review of ecclesial documents will delineate the current state of the question.

In the next two chapters I turn to Thomas's treatment of prophecy to provide the historical understanding necessary to address the case of Muhammad. The text of *DV* itself invites us to draw on Thomas for our study. Perhaps the most contested sentence in the constitution on the salvific character of Sacred Scripture cites Thomas's question on prophecy in *De veritate* (hereafter *DVer*).[37] If the Council Fathers themselves appealed to Thomas on prophecy while composing the constitution on revelation, so might we in composing a proposal about Muhammad's status as a prophet. In chapter 3 I examine Thomas's systematic works to develop a taxonomy of "prophecy." To understand Thomas on revelation, one should turn to his treatment of prophecy, for where he treats *revelatio* he explicitly writes about *prophetiae*.[38]

He does not build a theory of knowledge in these questions. Rather, he observes the varying instances of prophecy at work in Scripture and sketches a complex portrait of this phenomenon.

While for Thomas prophecy in the Hebrew Scriptures culminates in the words of John the Baptist announcing Jesus's arrival, Scripture itself attests both to unbelievers performing prophetic acts and to prophets after the death of Christ. Caiaphas, the Jewish high priest who accused Jesus, and the Roman soldiers who cast lots for his garments, for example, prophesied without knowing what they were saying and doing.[39] In the Acts of the Apostles, Agabus and the daughters of Philip prophesy.[40] Thomas notes that Scripture invites us to conclude that those who do not believe in Jesus can speak and act prophetically and that the early Christian community included prophets. Thomas goes even further than Scripture when he insists that prophecy is a permanent element of Church life: "At all times there have not been lacking persons having the spirit of prophecy, not indeed for the declaration of any new doctrine of faith, but for the direction of human acts."[41] The modern reader might draw from this claim that the prophets' role was diminished after the death of Jesus's last apostle, since prophets direct human acts rather than propose new doctrines of faith. It is, in fact, the exact opposite. For the medieval faithful, religious worship primarily consisted in practices. Religious belief was not first about assent to propositions of the faith, but rather about fidelity to a religious tradition. So "acts" are central to community belief. Thomas's claim, then, should be read in this light: While not proposing new doctrines for belief, prophets shape a community's religious practice. Chapter 3 will outline how Thomas's treatment of prophecy is elastic in its scope and yet cohesive in its inquiry. He utilized the data of Scripture to demonstrate that at the heart of prophecy was John the Baptist, pointing directly to Christ. But closer to the outer limits of prophecy stand all sorts of unlikely figures, among whom today we might consider Muhammad.

In chapter 4 I turn from the theoretical to the concrete, as I take up unexpected prophetic figures in Scripture and analyze the pertinent Thomistic biblical commentaries on these figures (central among these are Thomas's commentaries on Isaiah, Hebrews, and Corinthians).

Together chapters 3 and 4 reveal Thomas's effort at one and the same time to be true to the varied scriptural testimonies while also weaving together a cohesive understanding of the prophetic experience. These chapters highlight contextual differences, developments in thought, and persistent themes throughout the Thomistic corpus. The textual analysis of these chapters maps out Thomas's treatment of prophecy in preparation for our test case, Muhammad. These chapters open up creative possibilities for considering prophets beyond the walls of the Church.

Interpreting these ecclesial documents in light of Thomas on prophecy leads us to open up a new direction in Muslim-Christian dialogue by considering whether Muhammad, a seventh-century nomad, was a religious prophet. Fifty years ago, Karl Rahner noted that the prophetic element in the Church demanded theological reflection.[42] Most of this work on prophecy has been done in France, Germany, and Italy, but it has received little attention in English-speaking countries.[43] In chapters 3 and 4 of this book, while not offering a comprehensive study of prophecy in the Christian tradition, I draw from the writings of Thomas, bringing to light this neglected aspect of his work. Thomas offers a surprisingly supple and complex account of prophecy, one that has not received sufficient attention in the scholarly Thomist literature, especially in works written in English. In addition, this study draws on biblical commentaries that have been largely neglected in contemporary scholarship. In its method and approach, this book contributes to a growing movement in Thomistic scholarship, sometimes called "biblical Thomism" or "Ressourcement Thomism."[44]

Once I have opened up the theoretical question of Muhammad's prophecy in the first four chapters by marrying the claims made at Vatican II about Muslim belief and practice to Thomas's understanding of the role of prophecy in the church, in chapter 5 I examine the work of Christian theologians who have asked the question about Muhammad's prophecy. The first section of the chapter takes up the work of those thinkers who have found an affirmative answer to this question: Montgomery Watt, Hans Küng, Kenneth Cragg, and David Kerr. Each of these thinkers has spent decades engaging Muslim sources and scholarship. Each offers a model for considering Muhammad as a prophet. I critically analyze these theologians' approaches to this question and suggest an alternative model to those of these initial four that warrants further research. In the spirit of the medieval *quaestio*, the rest of the chapter addresses objections to the argument of this book that arise from two representative thinkers: Jacques Jomier, O.P., and Christian Troll, S.J., each of whom has dedicated his professional life to Christian theological work in Muslim contexts. These thinkers offer objections along two main lines.

The first states that a Christian assent to Muhammad as a prophet inevitably sounds to Muslim ears as if the Christian has declared submission to Islam. A belief in the prophecy of Muhammad is a belief in all that Islam teaches, including its anti-Christian elements.[45] Islam teaches that Muhammad's recitations are final and universal. A Christian could never accept that claim without ceasing to be a Christian. Particularly problematic is the fact that assenting to Muhammad's claim replaces Jesus's universality with the universality of Muhammad. Jesus becomes the forerunner, speaking to particular people at a particular time. A Muslim understanding of Muhammad, then, cannot be agreed to by Christians and cannot serve as a meeting-place for people of both faiths.[46] So the first objector understands "prophecy" in the full Muslim sense of the word.

The second line of objection argues that Muslims would and have reacted negatively to such a redefinition of prophecy, which resembles none of the thick theological claims they assume in the term "prophet." It does no good to redefine prophecy in such a way that it is unrecognizable to Muslims and then ascribe that "prophecy" to Muhammad. The second line of objection understands the term "prophet" to be emptied of its Muslim contents such that it becomes a third term that is unrecognizable to the religious other we are trying to engage.[47]

The concluding chapter draws on the practice of analogical reasoning in the theology of religious pluralism and shows that a term in one religion—in this case "prophecy"—can have purchase in another religious tradition. Chapters 3 and 4, in fact, show that a Christian understanding of "prophecy" is already fluid, *before* even stretching beyond its ecclesial walls. The documents of Vatican II claim that Christians and Muslims share an overlapping web of beliefs. In other words, they use religious terms in overlapping ways. It is my task in this book to follow the term "prophecy" from deep within one theological tradition and into another. I offer analogical reasoning here as the preferred practice. I conclude the chapter by recalling that the Catholic Church already has practices of spiritual discernment that have been applied to postcanonical divine encounters. I offer the unlikely category of "private revelation" here as a possible model for discerning what is true and holy in the Qur'an. These discernment practices are offered as a possible way into a concrete examination of Muhammad's prophethood—an examination that would involve another book-length project.

A contemporary reading of Thomas Aquinas on prophecy provides the groundwork for the constructive argument of this book: The spirit and letter of Vatican II lead us to consider Muhammad as in principle a religious prophet, a position that can find sound footing in the Catholic theological tradition. I claim neither that Thomas would have understood Muhammad as a prophet nor that he thought Islam was a true religion. Instead, drawing on Thomas's teaching on prophecy enables us to develop Vatican II's claims about Islam. The theoretical argument turns practical with the guidance of several Christian theologians who have long studied Muslim belief and practice. Just as the medieval *quaestio*'s objections help the student get to the heart of the inquiry, the fifth chapter's engagement with objectors recognizes that my argument inevitably leads to related questions that will demand their own extended research.

The past fifty years of Christian theologians' engagement with other faith traditions have provided a world of theological resources. In this project I take a necessary step beyond interreligious encounter to reexamine categories within the Christian tradition.[48] By laying the groundwork for examining the prophecy of Muhammad, this investigation turns to neglected resources within the Catholic theological tradition and argues that the Church has reasons to be open to the possibility of postbiblical revelations—including those that Muhammad received in Mecca and Medina. Traditionally, postbiblical revelatory events have been captured in the marginal category of "private revelation," most typically expressed in Marian apparitions.[49] Private revelation is a small part of a wider prophetic dimension in the church.

In this book I place Muhammad's prophecy within that wider dimension. In sum, the prophetic insights that are documented in the Qur'an can be viewed through Christian claims to truth, not in spite of them.

Recent political events both in this country and abroad have shown that there is a pressing need for Christians to understand Islam in a theologically serious way. The Catholic Church occupies a unique role as mediator in the complex dialogue between the world of Islam and the secular West since it shares many fundamental beliefs with both sides. In this book I urge that Muhammad be viewed within a Christian theology of revelation, not in an effort to relativize Scripture but instead to offer a dynamic model of Christian revelation that is attentive to the seeds of the Word that are planted beyond Christian communities. Under this model, postbiblical revelatory events like the ones that in principle could have occurred in seventh-century Arabia, without offering a new content of faith, might help Christians deepen their understanding of God and strengthen their religious practice.

CHAPTER TWO

The State of the Question

By all accounts, Vatican II marked a radically new openness to other faiths in general and Islam in particular. In these past fifty years since the close of the Council, we have witnessed the Church grappling with and developing that openness. During this same time, we have enjoyed an explosion of scholarship on the meanings, interpretations, and trajectories of the Council.[1] Vatican II frames the argument of this book, as it provides the launch pad from which to discuss Catholic Christianity's current relationship with Islam.

In this chapter I take cues from a collection of essays compiled in honor of John O'Malley's *What Happened at Vatican II* (2010), in which O'Malley suggests that we are ready to move to a further stage of interpreting the Council:

> Instead of examining the documents in isolation from one another, we are now ready to examine them as interdependent and ready to see how that interdependence is essential for interpreting them correctly. We move to a consideration of each document as in some measure an expression of larger orientations and as an integral part of a cohesive corpus, which is a result in large part of the documents' intertextual character. . . . They implicitly but deliberately cross-reference and play off one another—in the vocabulary they employ, in the great themes to which they recur, in the core values they inculcate, and in certain basic issues that cut across them.[2]

The Documents of the Council and Afterward: *Dei Verbum*

Among the sixteen documents of the Council, the four constitutions function somewhat like the four Gospel accounts: they provide the interpretive keys for the documents as a whole that came out of the Council. Even among the constitutions, *DV* plays a central role, as it offers the theological lens through which to read the other three more ecclesiological constitutions.[3] The very process of redacting *DV*, begun in the early days of the first session and promulgated only three weeks before the close of the Council, mirrored the deliberations on several issues related to the Catholic Church's interactions with the cultural currents of the time. The final vote on November 18, 1965, was taken on the seventh form of the document (2,344 *placet* and 6 *non placet*). This represented a radical turnaround for a constitution that twice required papal intervention to break through an impasse during the conciliar discussions.[4] Cardinal Ermenegildo Florit, when introducing the final draft of *DV* to the Council assembly, stated that the constitution "formed the very bond among all the questions dealt with by this Council. It sets us at the very heart of the mystery of the Church and at the epicentre of ecumenical considerations."[5] Writing about its centrality to the whole conciliar experience, Ormond Rush notes with the Doctrinal Commission that *DV* was somehow "the first of all the constitutions of this council, so that its Preface introduces them all to a certain extent."[6] *DV*, and especially its preface, holds a central place among the four constitutions. This preface was absent from the first draft of the constitution. Its inclusion represents a dramatic shift in the Council's understanding of Sacred Scripture by accentuating the divine invitation to a dialogue of salvation. This preface affirms:

> Hearing the word of God with reverence and proclaiming it with faith, the sacred synod takes its direction from these words of St. John: "We announce to you the eternal life which dwelt with the Father and was made visible to us. What we have seen and heard we announce to you, so that you may have fellowship with us and our common fellowship be with the Father and His Son Jesus Christ"

(1 John 1:2–3). Therefore, following in the footsteps of the Council of Trent and of the First Vatican Council, this present council wishes to set forth authentic doctrine on divine revelation and how it is handed on, so that by hearing the message of salvation the whole world may believe, by believing it may hope, and by hoping it may love.[7]

All consideration of Sacred Scripture and tradition are taken up within this context of the sweeping history of salvation. The scope is broadened to include our origin and end in God. Rush emphasizes the importance of this preface to the conciliar documents as a whole. We will see how important its inclusion is for our own argument. Four aspects of *DV* frame our reading of conciliar pronouncements on interreligious issues.

The Primacy and Scope of Divine Revelation

Already in the title of the constitution we note the shift toward an expansive understanding of divine revelation that had taken place during the Council discussions of the drafts. It begins with "on divine revelation" instead of "on sacred scripture."[8] The more fundamental theme of divine revelation sets the stage from within which Sacred Scripture is considered. In a literal sense, "*Dei verbum*" refers first and foremost to the eternal Word of the Father, which is made manifest both in the created order and in the Word made flesh. This divine Word invites creatures into Trinitarian fellowship whose response to this revelation is to listen and proclaim, for what is at stake is nothing short of salvation.[9]

Revelation is no longer considered primarily in verbal terms. Instead, it includes all the ways God has chosen to become manifest to humanity. *DV* makes clear that since "revelation takes place as history (and not just *in* history), it cannot be reduced to verbal and conceptual expressions, let alone to written texts."[10] Thinking of revelation in verbal terms means thinking of it principally as propositional statements to be adhered to in faith. Instead, in this constitution revelation means a set of complex historical events and developments. The cognitive aspects are only one part of a wider religious experience that is expressed through many mediums, including poetry, legislation, prophecy, and prayer.[11] It is no surprise, then, that the scriptural texts include each of these forms of written expression.

The preface that was not included in the original schema places revelation squarely in the expansive context of God's creation and call. "Revelation" here is set in its widest frame, as an invitation by God to a conversation with believers. It is situated on an eschatological plane from creation to the climax of the Christ event, to the pilgrim Church who anticipates the end of time. This understanding of revelation is cosmic in its reach and dynamic in its delivery. "Revelation," then, includes both the document that witnesses to the history of the people of Israel and the experience of the early Church community and, in a secondary sense, all things that recall the Creator.[12]

The Inner Relationship between Scripture and Tradition

While revelation is placed on the arc of creation, incarnation, redemption, and the age of faith, this constitution emphasizes its inner unity. In the constitution's own words: "The pattern of this revelation unfolds through deeds and words bound together by an inner dynamism, in such a way that God's works, effected during the course of the history of salvation, show forth and confirm the doctrine and the realities signified by the words, while the words in turn proclaim the works and throw light on the meaning hidden in them."[13] All the controversies from the initial schema around the two sources of revelation—Scripture and tradition—melt away. Each makes sense only in terms of the other. God, who is already manifest in the created order, became known to the Israelites in order to prepare the way for the Gospel. As *DV* explicitly frames it, tradition and Scripture here function "like a mirror in which the church, during its pilgrimage on earth, contemplates God, the source of all that it has received, until it is brought home to see him face to face as he is."[14] The use of "pilgrim church," a term taken from *LG*, accentuates a church on a journey toward a final end, for which there is much work still ahead.[15]

So Scripture and tradition form part of a reciprocal relationship in which both originate and travel together toward the same end: "For both of them [Scripture and tradition], flowing from the same divine wellspring, in a certain way merge into a unity and tend toward the same end."[16] The original Latin for the term "wellspring" is the rarer term "*scaturigo*" ("wellspring") rather than the more common "*fons*" ("source"). *Scaturigo* is a more dynamic and active term; it connotes a gushing forth rather than an ordered relationship.[17] While the interplay between tradition and Scripture is dynamic, it is also substantive. Together they form a single deposit of faith. Even with respect to the content of Sacred Scripture, the Council accentuates the dynamic act of revealing over the written content. In defining Scripture, it does not say, "*Sacra Scriptura est verbum Dei*" but rather "*Sacra scriptura est locutio Dei*." Sacred Scripture, then, is a living act, a speech (*locutio*) captured in the moment it is being put into writing.[18] The pilgrim Church is still in the process of recording and understanding that living word.[19] The process of redacting and compiling Scripture itself includes an important role for oral transmission. And yet the written word is also indispensable in the development of oral tradition. Tradition is not a set of truths that add information about God not found in Scripture. Rather, it is "the process, already present within Scripture itself, by which that life-giving dialogue between God and human beings is nourished and preached to succeeding generations."[20] Benedict XVI, when reflecting on *DV* in 2010, suggested that "the living Tradition is essential for enabling the Church to grow through time in the understanding of the truth revealed in the Scriptures."[21] *DV* does not settle all questions on the matter, but it properly emphasizes the dynamic cross-pollination that occurs between Scripture and tradition as the understanding of revelation unfolds across the span of salvation history.

Revelation's Trinitarian Structure

At its heart, revelation is Trinitarian. All revelation is rooted in the eternal Word of the Father, expressed in both creation and incarnation. Jesus Christ "completes the work of revelation and confirms it by divine testimony."[22] With this event, no new public revelation is to be expected before the end of time. In the words of René Latourelle, "Since God has spoken his only Word, complete and entire (insofar as we can grasp it in our earthly condition), what more could he say? Likewise, having given us his only Son, what more could he give us?"[23] Revelation as public manifestation, then, is complete. In a crucial way, nothing remains to be said.

But the fact that God has been perfectly expressed in Jesus of Nazareth does not mean that this expression was fully understood by his first companions, or by succeeding Christian generations. As *DV* puts it, "God's words, expressed through human language, have taken on the likeness of human speech, just as the Word of the eternal Father, when he assumed the flesh of human weakness, took on the likeness of human beings."[24] In other words, God chose to descend into the realm of human imperfection, "where the light of truth is sparse and must exist in the penumbra of partial knowledge mixed with partial ignorance."[25] The process of understanding who is the Christ documented in the Scriptures will remain incomplete until the end of time. This is why Scripture raises as many questions as it answers. While the revelation of Jesus Christ is perfect, complete, and whole, until the end of time the Church will move more deeply into encounter with and knowledge of Christ, bringing new questions to the scriptural text in every generation.

The Trinitarian structure of divine revelation means that the Spirit of Christ both perfects faith and brings about a deeper understanding of revelation such that we are better able to appropriate its message.[26] Faith, then, before being the acceptance of revealed truths, is first and foremost "the trusting human response to God's salvific invitation."[27] Under the guidance of the Holy Spirit, Christian believers grow in their understanding both of the words that have been handed down and of the realities that these words signify. *DV* explicitly states, "In this way the God who spoke of old still maintains an uninterrupted conversation with the bride of his beloved Son."[28] We will note how this conversation expands to include the religious other.

The Continuation of the Dynamic Appropriation of Revelation until the End of Time

We have already seen how *DV*'s reflections on divine revelation introduce us to a model in which Scripture recounts the history of the development of the relationship between God and the chosen people, a relationship that reached its apex in Jesus of Nazareth. But the Christian community's understanding and appropriation of this message is not yet complete. Two possible models for how this completion can take place should be considered.

One model is that of the "inspired reader." *DV* insists that Scripture, if approached in prayer, becomes "a dialogue [*colloquium*] between God and the human reader."[29] Many scriptural texts owe their development to a *"relecture"* (rereading of earlier texts). One could, in fact, argue that the whole of the New Testament is a practice in a Christian rereading of the Hebrew Scriptures. To provide just two examples, Daniel rereads an oracle in Jeremiah (Dan. 9 and Jer. 25:11–12), and St. Paul rereads Abraham's righteousness (Rom. 4:33 and Gen. 22:18–20). Within Scripture, we already notice that "inspiration" includes the actions of reading, rereading, and writing. Scripture itself invites readers into this process of rereading. Cardinal Vanhoye notes that "under the guidance of the Holy Spirit, [these inspired readers] not only discover the profound meaning of ancient texts, but contribute to them an addition to their meaning. Their action of reading includes an action of creativity."[30] This is clearly taking "inspiration" in a loose sense, such that no new biblical texts are introduced into the canon through this inspired reading. And yet inspired reading is called for if the biblical word is to become a living word in each age.

New Testament scholar and Anglican Bishop N. T. Wright offers another model, that of an unfinished play. We live in the fifth act, while the first four acts—that of Creation, the Fall, the call of Israel, and the ministry of Jesus—have already been performed. The first four acts offer "a world-view which, as someone comes into it and finds how compelling it is, quietly shatters the world-view that they were in already."[31] The New Testament forms the first scene of the fifth act, which in a real way will remain unfinished until the end of time. We train ourselves in the scriptural language and culture of the first four acts and then work out the remainder of the fifth act for ourselves. We are charged with living out the fifth act with innovation such that we bring to bear the language of the first four acts in our living moment. Yet we should also adhere to a consistency that maintains the narrative arc set by the initial acts. As a result, tradition, understood either in terms of inspired readers in the view of Cardinal Vanhoye or of creative actors as in that of N. T. Wright, provides the method of the argument of this book. The term "prophecy" within the text of Scripture has fields of meaning not yet harvested in the Church. New readings of the Bible by those who have encountered the religious other are possible with this method. The process of learning from the religious other becomes incorporated into the Christian's understanding of her own tradition, a process that will remain incomplete until the end of time.

Our analysis of *DV* highlights the dynamic model of revelation offered by this constitution. Its dynamism spreads from the process of the unfolding of revelation, the cross-pollination between Scripture and tradition, the Trinitarian invitation at the heart of revelation, and the incompleteness of this process until the end of time. *DV* recognizes the complete and perfect revelation in Jesus Christ, such that no new revelation could compete or be regarded on the same plane as Jesus Christ. But *DV* places this specific and climactic revelation in the context of the unfinished business of understanding that revelation. How is this pertinent to the theology of religious pluralism and interreligious dialogue? While the divine messages received in seventh-century Arabia could not be seen to compete with the revelation of Jesus Christ, they have the potential to help us unfold the truths of Scripture. Some of the questions that we bring to our reading of Scripture could have emerged only through contemporary challenges of interreligious conversation and did not form the explicit landscape of first-century Palestine, and yet when we return to Scripture armed with these new questions, we allow its living language to shape how we ask and answer our contemporary questions. And these contemporary questions have the potential to unlock new meanings in the scriptural text. This reading of *DV* will be brought to bear on an examination of *LG* and *NA*, as they apply this dynamic theology of revelation to a consideration of our encounter with non-Christians in general and Muslims in particular. This reading of *DV* also frames the theological practice of this book: My own interreligious encounters with Muslims led me to reexamine scriptural and theological categories in my tradition of inquiry and, ultimately, to the writing of this book.

LUMEN GENTIUM

Although *LG* affords Islam a smaller role than does *Nostra Aetate*, we will treat it first. Both postconciliar pronouncements and the redaction of the documents themselves encourage our ordering of this discussion. In 1984, the Synod of Bishops suggested a hermeneutical rule for interpreting the documents of the Council. They recommended that the four constitutions serve as the interpretive keys for the other decrees and declarations.[32] In addition, the process of redacting and promulgating also gives *LG* prominence. *LG* was promulgated toward the end of the third period of the Council (November 21, 1964). *NA* was revised during the fourth period, so those involved in the final revision were able to consult what already had been set forth officially in *LG*.

While *DV* frames human history as an invitation into the dialogue of salvation, *LG* specifies that this dialogue is ordered through the Church as the primary sign of salvation. Chapter 2 of *LG* considers all of humanity in relation to the Church, organized along two rings, one inside the other. The inner ring includes the Catholic faithful, catechumens preparing for reception into the Church, and other baptized Christians. The outer ring is composed of those who have not yet received the Gospel but who are ordered to the people of God. First among these are the Jews, who are the permanent recipients of the Abrahamic covenant, for "God never goes back on his gifts and his calling."[33] In the second layer of this ring stand Muslims, since they acknowledge the Creator. Arguably for the first time in the history of the Church, the magisterium makes the following claim about Muslims: "They profess to hold the faith of Abraham and along with us they worship the one merciful God who will judge humanity on the last day."[34] On the one hand, the Council claims that Muslims "profess" [*profitentes*] to hold the faith of Abraham, withholding judgment about whether this faith they profess *is* the same faith of Abraham that Christians profess.[35] Yet, in the same sentence the Council admits not only that Muslims adore the one [*unicum*] merciful God but that they adore this God *along with us* [*nobiscum*]. This is not a claim about coming to know the one God through reason. The God met in adoration is met in prayer, in religious ritual. This claim is then framed in eschatological terms, where both Christians and Muslims—together it seems—await the final day of judgment.

After the promulgation of *LG*, the crafters of *NA* could take certain theological assertions for granted. First, after the Jewish people, Muslims are afforded pride of place in the conciliar treatment of other religions. While leaving aside how Muslims are related to Abraham, Muslims and Christians together adore God, who is believed by both traditions to be merciful, one, creator and judge.[36] An early draft of *LG* acknowledged the Muslim claim to biblical and historic filiation to Abraham, but the final draft eliminated this recognition. The Council did not want to explicitly recognize that Muslims are sons of Ishmael and, in turn, implicitly include them in biblical revelation.[37] Since we "adore" this God together, this adoration is done for both traditions in the context of prayer and religious ritual. The words of this constitution imply that the God under discussion is not simply the Creator God known by natural reason, but rather the God revealed through the eyes of faith.[38]

Daniel Madigan pointedly notes that we cannot say that we worship one and the same God together and then "say that we cannot or may not talk together about that God, or about the sense of adoration that God evokes in us."[39] I would extend Madigan's point further to argue that, if Muslims and Christians honor the one God together, the sacred text that documents the summit of the encounter between Muslims and God should have something to say to Christians about the God we both worship.[40] For Christians, the Qur'an is not an alternative revelation alongside the revelation in Jesus Christ. The canon need not be reopened. But Madigan helpfully suggests that we replace ecumenical language referring to others as inside or outside the Church with language of direction and orientation.[41] This imagery follows neatly upon that of *LG* itself, with all of humanity ordered toward the Church. At the center of Christian faith stands the revelation found in Jesus Christ. But if *LG* is read intertextually in the context of *DV*, as John O'Malley has encouraged, we see that God establishes a dialogue of salvation with all of humanity. The Church is the primary sign and symbol of this dialogue, and, as a result, it provides the centerpiece. But *LG* adds concretely that if she is to listen to God attentively, she may want to learn from the ways that Muslims adore the one God. This means that while the Council remained pointedly silent about both the Qur'an and Muhammad, post-conciliar Christians may consider how each informs the dialogue of salvation outlined in *DV*. The project of this book is but one modest move in that direction.

To be sure, these groundbreaking claims about Muslims are framed in a missionary context, one in which "the Church prays and works at the same time so that the fullness of the whole world may move into the people of God, the body of the Lord and the temple of the Holy Spirit."[42] But even here we find a positive statement about the good among non-Christians. Whatever good "is found in people's hearts and minds, or in their particular rites and cultures [*propriis ritibus et culturis*], is not only saved from destructions but is made whole, raised up, and brought to completion to the glory of God"[43] through the Church. This is the first positive claim about non-Christian *religions* in the documents of Vatican II, as they simply reject an individualistic account of how God moves particular people toward salvation. The term "sown" (*seminatum*) recalls St. Justin's notion of "seeds of the Word," which became a recurring image in later conciliar documents.[44] While the Council took care not to endorse either the Qur'an or Muhammad, it did acknowledge that God works not just in individual non-Christians but through the particular rites and customs of their religious communities.

By the time *LG* was promulgated in 1964, the Council had already affirmed that, together, Muslims and Christians adore the one God who is merciful, creator, and judge. To this is added that the seeds of the Word are found not only in the minds and hearts of individual Muslims but also in their communal rituals and customs.

NOSTRA AETATE

NA, among the most contested Vatican II documents,[45] expands upon the positive claims made about non-Christian religions in *LG* in crucial concrete ways. It recognizes that religions outside Christianity address the "anxiety of the human heart" by offering "'ways,' that is, teachings and rules of life as well as sacred rites."[46] In other words, it speaks to the good that is present in non-Christian doctrines, moral teachings, and religious ritual. Aspects of what non-Christians believe, the manner in which they live, and how they choose to pray are highlighted here. If there were still any doubt that religious people encounter God through concrete teachings, practices, and rituals and not in spite of them, this doubt is laid to rest in the text of *NA* (although we will see how this doubt persisted in the years after the Council). This affirmation builds on the claims made in *LG* and clearly moves from an appreciation of individual non-Christians toward recognition of the beliefs and practices of their religious communities. These rules of life and sacred rites "frequently reflect a ray of that truth which enlightens everyone,"[47] and, as *NA* famously asserts: "The Catholic Church rejects nothing of those things which are true and holy in these religions."[48] The document does not outline how Catholics are to recognize non-Christian truth claims or encounters with holiness in other faith traditions, but it does leave open the possibility of this recognition or encounter. It left it to post-Conciliar Christians to turn this possibility into a reality. My argument in this book responds to this invitation.

What *NA* Asks of Catholics

On a practical level, *NA* asks Catholics to enter into dialogue and collaborate with followers of other religions in order to "preserve and promote those spiritual and moral good things as well as the sociocultural values which are to be found among them."[49] Note that here again *NA* encourages Catholics not just to work toward common social goods with followers of other faiths but also to collaborate with them to promote spiritual goods. *NA* goes on, then, to outline what these goods might be. With respect to Muslims in particular, the document affirms:

> They adore the one God, living and subsisting in Himself; merciful and all-powerful, the Creator of heaven and earth, who has spoken to men; they take pains to submit wholeheartedly to even His

inscrutable decrees, just as Abraham, with whom the faith of Islam takes pleasure in linking itself, submitted to God. Though they do not acknowledge Jesus as God, they revere Him as a prophet. They also honor Mary, His virgin Mother; at times they even call on her with devotion. In addition, they await the day of judgment when God will render their deserts to all those who have been raised up from the dead. Finally, they value the moral life and worship God especially through prayer, almsgiving and fasting.[50]

Remember that *LG* had highlighted four characteristics of God that Muslims and Christians acknowledge together: that He is one, merciful, creator, and judge. *NA* adds to these self-subsisting and all-powerful.[51] Each of these terms is both quranic and biblical. The Council took great care in choosing attributes of God that resonated with Muslims theologically but that were also doctrinally sound in a Christian context.[52] Muslims do not claim to arrive at these attributes of God through the use of their natural reason. Gavin D'Costa argues that both *NA* and *LG* imply "something more than natural theology in bringing back the Abrahamic typology," but he also acknowledges that the "Abrahamic typology clearly aligns Muslims with revelatory history in a typological manner rather than through a historic covenant."[53] In addition, it is crucial to notice that Muslims submit wholeheartedly to God's *inscrutable* decrees. This accentuates the aspect of mystery in Muslim faith, as Muslims understand themselves to be adhering to God in faith, not just through rational inquiry.[54] Note also that this God "has spoken" to human beings, but the question of how and through whom is left unresolved. We know that this was an intentional move on the part of the Council, since the members of the Theological Commission stopped these particularities from being included in the relevant text from *LG*. They did not want to give the impression that they had agreed that God had also spoken through Muhammad.[55] Both the constitution and the declaration limit themselves to the attributes of God. *DV* already specified that there has been no public revelation since the death of the last apostle. Robert Caspar, one of the crafters of *NA*, notes that since theological opinion on "revelation," broadly conceived at the time, was varied, the Council chose to remain silent on this issue.[56] The operating hermeneutic of the Council encouraged it to pronounce on areas of majority theological agreement.

Some readers of *DV* maintain that the paragraph under consideration (no. 3) refers to Muslims but not to Islam as a religion. It is important to note, then, that the subheading of this paragraph changed from *De Musulmanis* to *De religione islamica*. This change was made because the Council determined that they should deploy terminology used by Muslims. The theological consultants noted that when speaking about people the term "Muslim" should be applied, but when speaking about the actual religion the term "Islam" or "Islamic religion" should be used. Gavin D'Costa concludes, "This indicates without ambiguity that the religion, not just the anthropological human subjects in an act of worship, is the subject of these sentences."[57] D'Costa adds, however, that when the subheadings were removed at the final promulgation, this introduced the ambiguity of whether the document referred just to individual Muslims or to the religion as a whole that the Council members had previously taken pains to erase.

If, as *NA* explicitly affirms, Muslims and Christians honor the same God, and if, as the document readily acknowledges, Muslims and Christians share an overlapping web of beliefs, we should not be surprised to find the Qur'an to be a vehicle of grace in Muslim communities.[58] More importantly, if Muslims are being rightly guided by God through an encounter with the Qur'an, Christians should consider the possibility that this sort of interaction could bring Christians to a deeper appropriation of their own faith. Much like Marian apparitions that "bring the Gospel to life in a prophetic manner in new historic or geographic situations,"[59] qur'anic revelations, while not adding to the deposit of the faith, might enliven Catholics at a particular historical moment, helping them more fully to understand and live out the Gospel. While addressing what status these conciliar documents afford the Qur'an is a thorny and yet unresolved question, the task of this study takes up the related question of the prophetic status of Muhammad, upon whom the conciliar documents are resoundedly silent. Establishing in principle the possibility of the prophecy of Muhammad leads to the question of the status of the Qur'an. But, as we shall see, even the recognition in principle of Muhammad as a prophet does not lead to a wholesale adoption of the Qur'an. However, it does invite Christians to take the Qur'an theologically seriously as a document that contains seeds of the Word.

Most importantly, *NA*'s claims about non-Christians in general and Muslims in particular are a logical conclusion of the theology of revelation that emerges from *DV*. Remember that the Council decidedly conceptualized Scripture within the wider range of God's act of revealing. *DV* refers first and foremost to the eternal Word of the Father, which is made manifest both in the created order and as the Word made flesh. The "seeds of the Word" that are already found in creation are brought to their fulfillment in Christ. Our understanding of this Christian revelation is an ongoing process that will remain incomplete until the end of time. *DV* is clear that no new public revelation is expected after the death of the last apostle, but, as Michael Barnes, S.J., notes: "Revelation as the perfect instantiation of God's truth in Jesus Christ is closed; revelation as the ever-continuing process by which this truth becomes known in the world through the action of Word and Spirit together is not. *NA* laid down a principle, a corollary of what is taught in *DV*, that the Church does not reject the 'spiritual and moral good things' which may be found in other religions (*NA* 2)."[60]

Learning from other faith traditions, then, becomes woven into the fabric of coming to understand and appropriate Christian revelation. The dialogue of salvation into which God invites all of humanity is the setting for such work.[61] In his post-Synodal Apostolic Exhortation *Verbum Domini*, Benedict XVI spoke of the mystery of the Word that is constantly present in the Church by referring to *DV*. In doing so, he reaffirmed that "God, who spoke in the past, continues to converse with the spouse of his beloved Son. And the Holy Spirit, through whom the living voice of the Gospel rings out in the Church—and through it in the world—leads believers to the full truth and makes the word of Christ dwell in them in all its richness."[62] If, as *NA* and *LG* explicitly state, Muslims and Christians adore the one God together, the God who spoke definitively through Christ also might continue to speak to believers in many post-canonical and yet qur'anic ways. Remember that revelation closed with the last apostle, but unpacking the meaning of this revelation will continue until the end of time. Muslims believe that the same God who spoke through the Scriptures revealed the 114 chapters of the Qur'an to Muhammad. Catholics after Vatican II now recognize that Muslims and Christians share an overlapping web of beliefs. What are we to make, then, of the messenger of this divine *locutio*, Muhammad? How do we listen attentively to the seeds of the Word planted outside the Christian Scriptures and yet inside a history of salvation? This study considers the possibility that, in principle, Muhammad was a religious prophet, an argument that is constructed within a Christian theological framework.

Benedict XVI, in a forword to Niels Hvidt's seminal work *Christian Prophecy: The Post-Biblical Tradition* (2007), affirms that the prophetic element in the Church will remain a possibility until the end of time: "It seems clear to me that—considering the entire life of the Church which is the time when Christ comes to us in Spirit and which is determined by this very pneumatological Christology—the prophetic element, as element of hope and appeal, cannot naturally be lacking or fade away. Through charisms, God reserves for himself the right to intervene directly in the Church to awaken it, warn it, promote it, and sanctify it. I believe that this prophetic-charismatic history traverses the whole time of the Church."[63] This understanding of prophecy follows naturally from *DV*'s dynamic account of revelation delineated in the previous pages. We will see how well it accords with Thomas's account of prophecy in the next two chapters and how it coheres with the openness to the possibility of Muhammad's prophethood suggested in the ensuing chapters.

NA after the Council: The Past Fifty Years

NA expresses a fresh reconsideration of other faith traditions. In the decades following the Council, much theological reflection, taking cues from the conciliar documents, began working out answers to questions left undeveloped, thereby filling in gaps where the documents were silent.[64] *NA*, while certainly a groundbreaking document, explicitly referred to only three of the five pillars of Islam (presumably because the first pillar, witness [*shahâda*], and the last, pilgrimage [*hajj*], were too closely tied to Muhammad).[65] The Council was also silent on a wide range of issues concerning other religions. Mariasusai Dhavamony, S.J., professor emeritus at the Gregorian University, provides an illuminating list: "The Council did not wish to enter into discussion on the mode and the grade of belonging of religions to the history of salvation. It did not wish to pronounce on the content and nature of revelation contained in them, nor on the eventuality of their permanence until the end of the world. Besides, the Council says nothing on the historical origin of religion or religions, on the character of respective founders of religions, nor on the presence in them of elements of primitive revelation."[66] Even with a renewed openness to interreligious dialogue, the conciliar documents left unresolved the relationship between evangelization and dialogue. Summarizing the theological developments that emerged during the twenty years following the council, Jacques Dupuis concluded that the Church still needed to overcome explicitly "a long-standing habit of reducing evangelization to explicit proclamation and sacramentalization in the Church community, a task to which the promotion of justice and work for human liberation remains somehow peripheral and interreligious dialogue apparently foreign."[67] So the Council, while groundbreaking in its treatment of other religions, invited further theological research in order to delineate the full implications of its novel claims.

During the Council, Pope Paul VI created the Secretariat for Non-Christians, which was later renamed by Pope John Paul II in 1988 the Pontifical Council for Interreligious Dialogue (hereafter, PCID). This dicastery published *Guidelines for Dialogue between Christians and Muslims* initially in 1970, then revised and reissued the guidelines in 1981. Maurice Borrmans, a member of the White Fathers, director of the journal *Islamochristiana* (1975–2004) and for many years a member of the faculty at the Pontifical Instititute for Arab and Islamic Studies (hereafter, PISAI) in Rome, rewrote the *Guidelines* in coordination with suggestions from a group of consultors to the Secretariat for Non-Christians. These *Guidelines* were meant to provide Christians with basic knowledge of Islamic beliefs and practices in order to prepare them for dialogue with Muslims. The *Guidelines* also include accounts of the ideas of Muslims about Christianity, the possibilities of theological convergences, and areas for future collaboration. With respect to the issue of the prophecy of Muhammad, the *Guidelines* note that Christians should examine the "differing understandings of what is meant by prophecy in the fullest sense" and should assess "exactly what was the inspiration, the sincerity and the faithfulness of the Prophet Muhammad, making their judgment within the framework, first, of his personal response to the commands of God, and then, on a wider scale, that of the working of providence in world history."[68] The *Guidelines* suggest that, given their varying definitions of prophethood, neither Christians nor Muslims should require of the other everything that they understand by "prophet." They conclude by noting that Christians find in Muhammad "a great literary, political and religious genius, and that he possessed particular qualities which enabled him to lead multitudes to the worship of the true God;" however, they also find in Muhammad "evidence of certain mistakes and important misapprehensions"; most importantly, however, they *"also discern in him marks of prophethood."*[69] It is my aim in the next two chapters to work out what these marks could mean within a Catholic understanding of prophecy.

DIALOGUE AND PROCLAMATION

The need for further clarification of the relationship between evangelization and dialogue led to the publication in 1991 of *Dialogue and Proclamation* (hereafter, *DP*), published jointly by the PCID and the Congregation for the Evangelization of Peoples, with the approval of the Congregation for the Doctrine of the Faith (CDF).[70] It is offered as a reflection on and further specification of John Paul II's encyclical *Redemptoris missio* (nos. 55–57), issued six months earlier. This document brings together the threads of the conciliar reflections about dialogue, saying that *NA* speaks of the presence in these traditions of "a ray of that Truth which enlightens all" (*NA* 2). Another document of the Council, *Ad gentes* (hereafter, *AG*), recognizes the presence of "seeds of the word" in cultures before the advent of Christianity and points to "the riches which a generous God has distributed among the nations."[71] Also, *LG* refers to the good that is "found sown" not only "in minds and hearts," but also "in the rites and customs of peoples" (*LG* 17).[72] Reflecting on the conciliar texts, *DP* states: "The Council has openly acknowledged the presence of positive values not only in the religious life of individual believers of other religious traditions, but also in the religious traditions to which they belong" (*DP* 17). The question of who was being affirmed—whether individuals or whole communities—still remained a live issue for decades after the close of the Council. *DP*'s main contribution lies in its clarification of the relationship between interreligious dialogue and proclamation, which, "though not on the same level, are both authentic elements of the Church's evangelizing mission." In other words, "both are legitimate and necessary . . . intimately related, but not interchangeable" (*DP* 17).[73] Years later, in 2005, Benedict XVI confirmed the Church's commitment to dialogue with Muslims in particular during World Youth Day in Cologne. In no uncertain terms, he stated, "Interreligious and intercultural dialogue between Christians and Muslims cannot be reduced to an optional extra. It is in fact a vital necessity, on which in large measure our future depends."[74]

Anchoring interreligious dialogue in the heart of evangelization means that Christians must allow themselves to be challenged by encounters with the religious other. The document gingerly states, "Notwithstanding the fullness of God's revelation in Jesus Christ, the way Christians sometimes understand their religion and practice may be in need of purification" (*DP* 32). In the process of evangelizing, Christians must always recognize that they do not fully grasp the truth: "In the last analysis truth is not a thing we possess, but a person by whom we must allow ourselves to be possessed" (*DP* 49). The document echoes here the comprehensive model of revelation given years earlier in *DV*. Evangelization, then, is a dynamic and unending process in which the evangelizer becomes evangelized herself in her encounter with the religious other. The unfolding process of revelation accentuated in *DV* now firmly includes interreligious dialogue.

DOMINUS IESUS

Some thirty-five years of absorbing the spirit of *NA* into theological reflections led to the publication of *Dominus Iesus* (hereafter, *DI*) in 2000. With unyielding clarity, this declaration sharply poses the question of how the Church can acknowledge what is true and holy in other religions in a way that preserves the absolute truth and salvific universality of Christ.[75] *DI* claims to be a boundary-setting document for all those theologians who work *ex corde ecclesiae*, outlining the "indispensable elements" of Christian faith that must be preserved in any theology of religious pluralism.[76] *DI* enumerates the foundational cornerstones of the faith:

> The definitive and complete character of the revelation of Jesus Christ, the nature of Christian faith as compared with that of belief in other religions, the inspired nature of the books of Sacred Scripture, the personal unity between the Eternal Word and Jesus of Nazareth, the unity of the economy of the Incarnate Word and the Holy Spirit, the unicity and salvific universality of the mystery of Jesus Christ, the universal salvific mediation of the Church, the inseparability—while recognizing the distinction—of the kingdom of God, the kingdom of Christ, and the Church, and the subsistence of the one Church of Christ in the Catholic Church. (*DI* 4)

At the same time, however, *DI* recognizes the need for much theological reflection in this area; it urges, though, that these reflections be undertaken with due care for the central mysteries of Christian faith and experience. Its contribution to the contemporary conversation on religious pluralism lies not in any constructive proposal, but rather in its reiteration of central Christian convictions. *DI* insists that any theological proposal that puts the sacred documents of other religions on a par with Christian revelation denies the definitive and complete character of the revelation of Jesus Christ. Much scriptural testimony is marshaled to support the claim that the "Christian dispensation . . . as the new and definitive covenant, will never pass away, and we now await no further new public revelation before the glorious manifestation of our Lord Jesus Christ" (*DI* 5). The revelation of Jesus Christ is full, true, complete, and perfect. The act of revelation calls forth an assent of faith on the part of the believer (*DI* 7).

    DI then offers a provocative—but underdeveloped—distinction between *theological faith*, on the one hand, and *belief* of people in other religions, on the other. Theological faith is the acceptance of the truth revealed by God. Belief, by contrast, is "that sum of experience and thought that constitutes the human treasury of wisdom and religious aspiration, which man in his search for truth has conceived and acted upon in his relationship to God and the Absolute." But it is "religious experience still in search of the absolute truth and still lacking assent to God who reveals himself."[77] *DI* here seems to close the door to the possibility, originally opened by *NA*, that truth can be found in other religions, but in the very next paragraph that door is reopened. *DI* insists that the sacred writings of other religions cannot be called "inspired texts," as "the church's tradition . . . reserves the designation of *inspired texts* to the canonical books of the Old and New Testaments, since these are inspired by the Holy Spirit" (*DI* 8). And yet God "'does not fail to make himself present in many ways, not only to individuals, but also to entire peoples through their spiritual riches, of which their religions are the main and essential expression'" (ibid., quoting *Redemptoris missio* no. 55). Note that God works not only inwardly on individual non-Christians but also outwardly reveals himself through their religious traditions. But how can God become present to other religions without calling forth assent on the part of religious people? In the words of Francis Clooney:

> Given the declaration's explanation of faith as a "personal adherence of man to God," . . . the denial of "faith" to the people of other religious traditions must be interpreted as also indicating that in other religious traditions there can be no relationship with God of the sort that counts as that personal adherence which is also faith. . . . If God is present to people in their own religions, God is surely present in such a way that those people can respond to God and adhere to God even before assenting fully to revelation as understood in the teachings of the Roman Catholic Church.[78]

Clooney is looking for stronger language to account for other religious believers' assent to God. In addition, *DI* 8 states that the sacred books of these traditions ultimately receive from the mystery of Christ their elements of grace and goodness. But James Fredericks poses this question: "If the grace contained in the Sutras and the Upanishads, the Qur'an, and the Dao-de-jing is from Christ and not merely the product of human wisdom untouched by grace, how then can Christians maintain a stark, un-nuanced distinction between 'theological faith,' on the one hand, and 'belief, in the other religions,' which is merely 'that sum of experience and thought that constitutes the human treasury of wisdom and religious aspiration?' True, *DI* sets clear boundary markers around dogmatic claims that call forth theological faith, but it also invites exploration around this category of "belief" that arises in other religions. *DI* reflects rather than resolves the tension found in *NA* 35 years earlier. Both documents seek to affirm the definitive revelation in Christ without denying God's presence beyond the walls of the Church, and yet neither document fully accounts for how this could take place. The argument of this book seeks to explore this category of "belief" that arises in other religious traditions in a way that would satisfy both the demands of *DI* and the concerns posed by its two critics named here.

Taking the conciliar documents and the postconciliar magisterial reflections as the springboard from which to pursue this inquiry, we must ask ourselves whether Muhammad's revelatory experiences in Mecca and Medina have a place within a Christian understanding of revelation. While Christians affirm that the Christ event is the perfect fulfillment of revelation, is postbiblical understanding of revelation open to the angel Gabriel's revelations to Muhammad? Given that revelation closed with the death of the last apostle, the Qur'an could not be considered revelation on a par with Christian revelation. But the understanding of revelation framed in *DV*, read through the claims about Muslims in *LG* and *NA*, leaves open the possibility that the messages emerging from Muhammad's encounter with the angel Gabriel might help Christians understand revelation more fully at a particular moment in history.

We turn, then, to the one chosen to receive these diving messages, Muhammad. Vatican II claims that Christians and Muslims adore the one God together. What are we to make of the prophet who communicates God's message to one-fifth of the world's population? Given the overlapping web of beliefs between Christians and Muslims affirmed by the Council, we ask ourselves how God chose Muhammad to be the vehicle to communicate a divine message. Christians need to find language that properly acknowledges this possibility. The current proposal argues that Muhammad could, in principle, be considered a religious prophet. But to make this novel argument, we must analyze what "prophecy" means in the Christian tradition. Who better to turn to at this juncture than its foremost representative medieval figure, Thomas Aquinas? The next two chapters will draw from his systematic works and biblical commentaries in order to present a portrait of "prophecy" that might be used to capture the features of Muhammad's encounter with God.

CHAPTER THREE

Thomas Aquinas on Prophecy

This chapter and the next sketch Thomas's analysis of prophecy, first by attending to his systematic treatments of this issue in the *De veritate* (*DVer*), *Summa contra gentiles* (hereafter, *ScG*), and *Summa theologiae* (hereafter, *ST*), and then by turning to his scriptural commentaries and systematic works that take up prophetic biblical figures (central among these are his commentaries on Isaiah, John, Hebrews, and Corinthians).[1]

These chapters serve both a symbolic and a substantive function. Turning to a medieval figure, especially one so central to Christian thinking and practice as Thomas Aquinas, highlights the fact that our main argument is drawn from deep within the tradition of Christian theology. Substantively speaking, Thomas's account of prophecy offers a surprisingly subtle understanding of this complex phenomenon, one that opens itself up organically to the animating question of this book. In addition, most prior treatments of Thomas on this topic have attended either to the historical context or to a philosophical analysis of those with whom Thomas engaged.[2] Principal among Thomas's interlocutors was the Rabbi Moses Maimonides, but the Islamic philosopher Ibn'Sina and Thomas's own teacher, Albert the Great, also provided rich material for his consideration.[3] Thomas's treatment of prophecy emerges in conflict and conversation with these figures.[4] This account of prophecy has been marshaled into several sides of twentieth-century debates concerning biblical inerrancy and scriptural inspiration.[5] Important work has been written on his treatment of prophecy in these areas, and these chapters will draw on those studies where appropriate.

Our argument applies Thomas's discussion of prophecy to a pressing contemporary issue in the theology of religious pluralism. The textual analysis of these chapters maps out his account in preparation for our test case on religious prophecy: Muhammad. We propose to apply his analysis of prophecy to our contemporary question of whether Muhammad's message has any bearing for Christians, and we knowingly take Thomas's work where he would not have taken it.

We turn briefly to the four places in Thomas's corpus where he mentions Muhammad. In a section in the *ScG* where he discusses how it is reasonable for Christians to assent to those truths of the faith above human reason, Thomas ushers in Muhammad as a counterexample. He had claimed in this section that Christianity is true for a catalogue of reasons: (1) the early Christian community believed in Jesus despite persecution and tyranny, (2) even the simple among them were filled with the gift of the Holy Spirit to believe truths that their minds were not able to reach and curb their sensual appetites, (3) many miracles were performed to attest to these truths, and finally, (4) the events recounted in the New Testament fulfilled the prophecies of the Hebrew Scriptures.

The experience of the early Muslims is offered as a counterexample, for they were seduced both by Muhammad's promises of carnal pleasures and by the "truths that he taught mingled with many fables and with doctrines of the greatest falsity."[6] Muhammad brought forth no supernatural signs. Instead, he relied on military power to spread his false messages. Thomas even claims that from the very beginning no wise men believed in Muhammad. Only brutes and desert wanderers who were ignorant of any divine truths believed in Muhammad. Thomas concludes by stating both that Muhammad perverted almost all of Christian scriptures and fabricated his own and that those "who place any faith in his words believe foolishly."[7]

Although Thomas is not explicitly arguing against Muhammad's prophethood *qua* prophethood here, given what he states both about Muhammad and about Islam, he would certainly not include Muhammad among the Hebrew Prophets. He mentions Islam only as a counterexample to his main argument as a way to contrast true and false religion. But again, his implicit conclusion here, of course, is that Muhammad was not a true prophet. Thomas very briefly mentions Muhammad in three other places in his corpus. In each instance he assumes that Muhammad is an apostate who spread his message by the force of arms and an appeal to carnal pleasures.[8] Thomas's assumptions about both Muhammad and Islam were widely shared at the time; one of his brothers fought in the Crusades, and it would have been unusually countercultural of him to think in any other way about Muhammad.[9] What Christians have learned about Muslim belief and practice in the seven hundred years that separate us from Thomas is analogous to what we have learned of human biology, astronomy, or history, to name just a few examples. The following chapters draw from Thomas's sophisticated account of prophecy without subscribing to his otherwise widely shared medieval caricatures of Muhammad and early Muslim believers.

Instead of beginning from the theoretical and then applying a theory of prophecy to particular prophetic moments, Thomas observes the varying instances of prophecy at work in Scripture and sketches a complex portrait of this phenomenon. Throughout the discussion of these questions on prophecy, one gains a sense of Thomas as the preacher who regularly wrote homilies on Scripture and the teacher who prepared young Dominicans to hear confessions and to preach in the emerging European urban centers of the thirteenth century.

While prophecy in the Hebrew Scriptures culminates in the words of John the Baptist announcing Christ's arrival, Scripture itself attests both to unbelievers performing prophetic acts and to scriptural figures speaking prophetically after the death of Christ. The Jewish high priest, Caiaphas, who accused Jesus, and the Roman soldiers who divided his garments, for example, prophesied without knowing what they were saying or doing.[10] In the Acts of the Apostles, Agabus and the daughters of Philip prophesied after the death of Jesus.[11] Scripture itself invites us to conclude that those who do not believe in Jesus can prophesy and that the early Christian community included prophets. Thomas goes even further than Scripture when he insists that prophecy is a permanent element in Church life: "At all times there have not been lacking persons having the spirit of prophecy, not indeed for the declaration of any new doctrine of faith, but for the direction of human acts."[12] These chapters will outline how Thomas's treatment of prophecy is both elastic and cohesive in scope. Thomas uses the data of Scripture to demonstrate that at the heart of prophecy lies John the Baptist, pointing directly to Christ. But closer to the borders of the prophetic instinct stand all sorts of unlikely figures. While Thomas would not have done so, we suggest the possibility of including Muhammad among these figures.

This chapter will outline Thomas's treatment of prophecy in his systematic works, noting any shifts in emphases or developments in thought on this topic. In the next chapter, we pinpoint a few representative prophetic figures from the Scriptures to highlight how prophecies can be delivered through unexpected people and in unanticipated ways. We analyze Thomas's reflections upon these figures' prophetic words and actions. Only then are we ready to make some preliminary observations about whether Muhammad fits into the prophetic mold shaped by Thomas.

THOMAS ON CHRISTIAN PROPHECY: A WEB OF FAMILY RESEMBLANCES

In order to prepare the groundwork for our analysis of Muhammad and Christian prophecy, we must turn back toward the medieval tradition and its foremost representative theologian. For an analysis of Thomas's systematic works, we look to the *DVer*, the *ScG*, and the *ST*, where he attempted to bring order and coherence to disparate biblical instances of prophecy.

Prophecy emerges out of a relationship between the teacher, the student, and the knowledge imparted between them. As in so many other parts of Thomas's corpus, pedagogy is his primary concern. This should come as no surprise, since he dedicated his life to teaching university students and Dominican friars. The pedagogical relationship between teacher and student sets the framework for his treatment of prophecy, so we will examine this relationship from various angles.

There are as many differences among prophetic revelations as there are among pedagogies. The teacher adapts her strategies to meet the subject matter at hand, the natural abilities of the student, and the teaching environment. Thomas finds that the same holds true in the prophetic realm. In this realm, however, there is a double pedagogical movement in which God imparts particular knowledge to a prophet, and then the prophet in turn becomes the teacher who admonishes or encourages those in her community about their relationship with God.

In the *ST* in particular, the treatment of prophecy is set within the context of *sacra doctrina*, or holy teaching.[13] In fact, one could say that this is the main concern of the work as a whole. The questions on prophecy are framed within this wider context and governed by earlier discussions about the various ways the human person comes to know God. In particular, Question One of *ST*, which serves as a prologue to the whole work, provides much of the background of the four questions on prophecy in the *Secunda secundae*.

A reader familiar with the *ST* will remember that in the opening article of the entire work, *sacra doctrina* is deemed necessary for the salvation of the human race; the same framework is operative here, as prophecy is needed for nothing less than salvation.[14] God desires that humans come to know Him. In fact, our eternal fulfillment consists in this knowledge. While some people who are privileged with acute intelligence, a lot of time for study, and the ability to take care of their day-to-day concerns do arrive at knowledge of God after a long time (even as this knowledge is riddled with errors), most need help to reach the knowledge of God that is our true end. God provides this help through the revelation that began with the song of creation, continued with the prophecies imparted to the Israelites, and climaxed in the person of Jesus Christ. Even after Jesus walked the streets of Nazareth, Christians still need help both to come to understand this embodied revelation and to live out its costly demands. Prophets began to assist in this dynamic process of revelation from the moment the Jews became a covenanted people. Moses, the most important prophet from the Hebrew Scriptures, established the law on Mount Sinai as a result of prophetic knowledge. The whole of Christian faith, in fact, rests on the revelations made to the apostles and prophets who wrote the canonical books.[15] Prophets continue to proclaim during the "age of grace" and will until the end of time, when we will know God not by hearing or in a piecemeal fashion, but rather through face-to-face encounter in the beatific vision.

The final aspect of *sacra doctrina* that sets the context for Thomas's treatment of prophecy is the inclusion of singulars in this *scientia*. In an ultimately unsatisfactory answer to an objection about how *sacra doctrina* is not a *scientia* because it treats of singulars like the deeds of Abraham, Isaac, and Jacob, Thomas replies that *sacra doctrina* does not principally deal with singulars. Instead, individual facts emerge only as examples to be followed in our lives and to establish the authority of those through whom the divine revelation has come down to us. *Sacra doctrina* is based on this revelation. For Aristotle, *scientia* trades in universals, not singulars. The mutability of singulars proves unstable for knowledge needed in *scientia*. Only universals are intelligible and provide the knowledge that moves from established principles to necessary conclusions. Thomas's argument that *sacra doctrina* is a form of *scientia*, then, has to be taken in a secondary sense. He settles on the term *subaltern scientia*, in that the first principles of this body of knowledge are found in God's knowledge of God's self and the knowledge that the blessed have of God.[16] This knowledge is imparted primarily through persons in history and only secondarily through intellectual arguments. Prophets, then, confirm scriptural revelation, but they themselves are also the transmitters of this revelation. They partake in the dynamic process of revelation, a process that did not end with the closing of the canon. While knowledge of God is true "*cognitio*," we are drawn to our final end through particular and concrete events and persons. *Sacra doctrina* does not strictly adhere to the principles of an Aristotelian *scientia*. Instead, it properly reflects the historicity of this body of knowing. This historicity, though, is ultimately subsumed into the God who has no beginning and no end.

Prophecy, then, is placed within an eschatological framework spanning the time of Abraham through the present and into the future. Rooted in Christ's Incarnation, it points toward the eschatological fulfillment of His Incarnation at the end of time. Prophecy is one way of coming to know God. Other avenues to knowledge of God are natural reasoning, hearing through faith, and seeing in the beatific vision. Each way of knowing God enjoys a particular light, be it the light of nature (*lumen naturae*), the light of faith or grace (*lumen fidei vel gratiae*), or the light of glory (*lumen gloriae*). Prophecy can be understood only as a part of humanity's journey to understand and love God. Ultimately, it serves the light of faith. Even if it fits uncomfortably in an Aristotelian *scientia*, it imparts certain knowledge of contingent particulars that are far from human knowledge. Having established that prophecy is a way of knowing, a *cognitio*, that is part of a larger web of coming to know God, let us look at the subject matter that comprises such knowledge.

PROPHECY 101: THE SUBJECT MATTER

While common parlance assumes that prophecy denotes knowledge of future events, Thomas's treatment reaches much beyond this limited account.[17] For him, prophecy is "a kind of knowledge impressed under the form of teaching on the prophet's intellect by Divine revelation."[18] In other words, it is a cognoscitive gift consisting in an illumination of the intellect (*lumen propheticum*) in order to judge the truth of something that is far (*procul*) from the reaches of human reason.[19]

Already in the prologue to the treatise on prophecy in the *ST*, Thomas sketches the scope of prophecy to include all things pertaining to knowledge. He explicitly denies that prophecy extends only to future events, but rather emphasizes that all things relating to God that surpass human knowledge can be the subject matter of prophecy. These include everything to be believed by faith, especially the direction of human acts. As a result, anything touching upon knowledge or love of God is a candidate for prophecy.

But prophetic knowledge must exclude anything false, for the knowledge of the disciple is a likeness to the knowledge of the teacher.[20] It is impossible for anything false to be taught by means of prophetic knowledge, as God is the teacher here. God's infallible knowledge imparts the prophecy. At root, this process of knowing is Trinitarian, as the prophet, whose mind is made into a likeness of the divine mind, ultimately participates in the person of the Son. Thomas writes in his *Commentary on John*: "At one time, the only Son of God revealed knowledge of God through the prophets, whose proclamation was measured to the extent to which they had been made participants in the eternal Word."[21]

The same Trinitarian pattern that is at work in *sacra doctrina* is operative in prophetic knowledge. Prophets are invited—however briefly—into the Trinitarian pattern of knowing. We will see that the prophet can choose to misunderstand, misuse, or ignore this knowledge, but the truth of the imparted knowledge cannot err. Prophets can also have a difficult time untangling what is knowledge of divine origin from what in fact is their own invention. But true prophecy emerges from divine knowledge, which is, of course, infallible.

Since God is the primary teacher, the prophet enjoys certitude about what she knows through prophecy. In a natural act of knowledge, a person is made certain of the first principles of cognoscitive judgment. In a parallel way, the prophet is certain about what she understands through the elevation of supernatural light. This certainty is needed for the sure impartation of this knowledge to others, for prophets cannot present things to others with assurance if they do not have certain knowledge of these things.[22]

Having established that prophecy is a cognoscitive gift of something pertaining to knowledge of God that is far from the reaches of reason, and that this process of knowing is ultimately Trinitarian in nature, we now turn to the particular grace at work in this knowledge. Prophecy is listed among the gratuitous graces, as these are bestowed by the Holy Spirit and given for the benefit or holiness of others.[23] The other gratuitous graces include wisdom, knowledge, miracles, discernment of spirits, tongues, and interpretation of speeches.[24] A person who receives a gratuitous grace is not sanctified in the process, but rather enjoys a freely bestowed gift for the benefit of other people. As a result, prophecy is naturally geared toward community. While Thomas spends a lot of time discussing how prophetic knowledge is imparted to the individual person, the structure of this knowledge is directed not toward the interior of the person but to the listening community as a whole. This is further accentuated by the inclusion of speech and miracles in this discussion of prophecy. Prophecy primarily concerns knowledge, but it also includes speech, as the prophet declares what she was taught by God for the instruction of others, and sometimes miracles, which confirm the divine origin of these revelations.[25] Because prophetic knowledge surpasses the reaches of the human intellect, it cannot be confirmed by any rational demonstrative principles. Miracles stand in the place of these rational demonstrations and serve as confirmation that the prophetic knowledge in question is of divine origin.[26]

Prophets share the truth received with others and point beyond themselves back to their root, which is found in God's diffusive goodness.[27] This process entails a participation in God's own sharing of His Truth and Goodness. The setting is pedagogical, as the prophet is enlightened in order to teach others, much as the grace of knowledge or wisdom is received by teachers. Thomas distinguishes here between knowledge and wisdom considered as gifts of the Holy Spirit whereby the person is moved interiorly by the Holy Spirit to know something of divine things on the one hand, and wisdom or knowledge on the other as gratuitous graces by which a person is enabled to instruct others and overcome adversaries of the faith.[28] In the teaching example, a teacher receives the gift of knowledge in order to impart it to her students. She could be corrupt in all sorts of ways. That knowledge might not transform her inwardly, and yet it is classified as a grace because it is given to her in order to enlighten others. Her interior life is independent of this gift. In prophetic knowledge, the emphasis is on the teaching, the impartation of knowledge, rather than on the interior movement of the Holy Spirit on the person. The Holy Spirit moves the person to speak or act on a particular occasion, while the person is not necessarily transformed in the process. The prophet is used as an instrument of the Holy Spirit for others, but the Holy Spirit does not take root in the prophet during this double pedagogical movement. We will see how the fact that prophecy is a gratuitous rather than a sanctifying grace becomes crucial in Thomas's discussion of unlikely prophetic figures in Scripture.

Since the subject matter of prophecy is so expansive and the prophetic grace is designed to be instructive for others, those governing the community draw upon the work of prophets. These teachers help steer its members in the aspects of knowledge of God that are beyond natural reason. Thomas explicitly mentions divine worship (*cultum divinum*) as a practice that benefits from prophetic guidance.[29] Remember that for Thomas *cultus* is the object of religion. Religion is considered under justice, which is the highest moral virtue. Virtues are habits that make a person good. Nothing sanctifies a person more than religion, since it renders to God what is due to God. Thomas goes so far as to equate religion (what we would call worship) to sanctity.[30] So prophets have an integral role to play in the central act of a Christian community: the liturgical and sacramental rituals that by being directed toward God sanctify the worshiping community. While divine worship is the summit of a religious community's belief and practice, prophecy is also necessary for the general instruction of the faithful and the formation of morals.[31] The whole of prophecy, in fact, is directed toward the virtuous life.[32] Much as in the case of *sacra doctrina*, the scope of prophecy is wide-ranging, as it can include anything that directs the human person to her final end in the beatific vision. Like *sacra doctrina* again, it is always directed toward a community of persons seeking to come to know and love God.

While the framework is pedagogical, the recurring metaphor throughout both the systematic and the scriptural commentaries is that of apparitions or manifestations. Thomas suggests two etymological roots of "*prophetia*."[33] One is found in Samuel 9:9 (*qui nunc dicitur propheta olim videns dicebatur*),[34] which is based on the Greek word φανός (*phanos*) and means "luminous," "visible," or "manifest." Another etymological root, the author of which Thomas claims was Isidore of Seville (*Etym.* VII.8), translates into *prae-fatores*. This means those who speak of things that are present and that will be into the future. But the Greek word προφήτης in the Septuagint comes from προφημί, meaning "to interpret." It can indicate a person who is "called" to a special task (*vocatus*) or a person who speaks (*vocans*) in the place of God.[35] Etymologically speaking, then, prophecy means a person who is called to speak in the place of God in order to make something manifest or visible about God. The end of prophecy is the manifestation of truth that surpasses human reason for the good of the ecclesial community. The clearer the manifestation, the more excellent the prophecy.[36] But even the most excellent prophecy will leave its listeners asking further questions, as prophecies do not ultimately satisfy the human intellect. Paul Rogers puts it this way: "Light of prophecy cannot be interpreted as an arrival of any sort, and it pales in comparison to the light of glory."[37] While prophecy entails a manifestation of something that had been hidden or an illumination of something that had been in the shadows, fundamentally it remains enigmatic until the end of time. The manifestation at work in prophecy is still very much *in via*. For at the end of time we will learn not by hearing through faith in bits and pieces. Instead, our hopes will be fulfilled; all that will remain is charity.

This metaphor reflects Thomas's wider conviction that God desires to manifest Himself from the beginning of time through creation. This desire to reveal Himself culminates in the Incarnation and yet is not complete until the beatific vision, in which we will see God face to face. This theological conviction is upheld by a deep metaphysics of *esse* throughout Thomas's work, where the God who seeks to meet human persons in history is complete and dynamic; this God fully *is*, *has been*, and *will be* without change or movement, without becoming from potency to act. This is a God who seizes every channel to make Himself known to creatures, a God who not only becomes human in order to meet creatures in the flesh, but also chooses the most unlikely people throughout history to communicate Himself to the faithful. Prophets assist the faithful during their journeys by encouraging them to remain true to God's promise and by admonishing them when they turn away from this promise.

All glimpses of God—be they through nature or grace—are preliminary moments that will find rest in the *visio* of the beatific vision.[38] In the beatific vision, this *visio* is emptied of its ocular connotations as the beatified come to know as God knows, not through any likeness or image. The *visio* of the beatific vision is impossible for the wayfarer to achieve through knowledge, whether by nature, grace, or even prophecy; in all these, one "sees" divine things through certain images.[39] Prophetic vision is not the vision of the very essence of God, and prophets do not see the divine essence Itself in the things they see; rather, they see through certain images (*quibusdam similitudinibus*) insofar as they are enlightened by the divine light.[40] While prophecy is a special knowledge bestowed only on certain individuals for the good of the community, the limitations set in place by virtue of being human are still operative. Even as the natural abilities of prophets are deepened and strengthened, ultimately they do not know as God knows.

The more excellent the manifestation, the deeper the prophecy. Inevitably, though, this knowledge is partial, transitory, hidden, and imperfect. It is knowledge that is remote from most of us,[41] it is received piecemeal,[42] and it is shadowy and mixed with darkness.[43] Prophecy is considered something imperfect in the genus of divine revelation. Placed within its proper eschatological framework, all prophecies will be made void at the end of time (1 Cor. 13:8). For now, we prophesy in part or imperfectly: "When that which is perfect is come, that which is in part shall be done away with. Consequently, it does not follow that nothing is lacking to prophetic revelation, but that it lacks none of those things to which prophecy is directed."[44] In other words, prophecy *by its very nature* is imperfect and incomplete. In his commentary on St. Paul's Letter to the Corinthians, Thomas specifies that prophetic knowledge is figurative and enigmatic and that it will be replaced by the clarity of vision in heaven.[45] Both partial and piecemeal knowledge of prophecy and knowledge gained through the gift of faith share the feature of being incomplete and inchoate.

Growth in the Christian life primarily concerns the development of the theological virtues of faith, hope, and charity. These take root and develop into habits that direct human living. But other effects are necessary, not for a whole life, but for definite times and places, such as when working miracles, foretelling future events, and the like. Thomas states that habitual perfections are not necessary for these actions but that "certain impressions are made by God, which cease to exist as soon as the act stops, and these impressions have to be repeated when the act is again to be repeated."[46] The prophet's mind is illumined by a new light for each revelation and in each case of performance of a miracle, for a new influence of the power of God is at work.

We have seen that, much like *sacra doctrina*, prophecy can include anything that relates to God. But it is more limited than *sacra doctrina* insofar as prophetic knowledge will almost always surpass the abilities of human reason. It is a truth revealed to a select person for the good of the wider community. Prophecy is always at the service of this community and directs its members toward the final end of all human living found in the beatific vision. But it comes piecemeal, in fragments, and in figurative dress. It is designed for the wayfarer *in via* but is ultimately meant to be replaced by the clarity of the beatific vision. What distinguishes prophecy from other ways of knowing is the process by which the truth is manifested. It is to this process that we now turn.

Prophecy 201: The Prophetic Experience

Considering that the subject matter of prophecy is always beyond the reaches of reason, how does the prophet attain such knowledge? The prophet cannot receive this revelation through the natural light of her intellect. As a result, the Holy Spirit raises the intention of the mind to perceive divine things, preparing the prophet to receive the revelation of God.[47] This supernatural light is not in the prophet by way of an abiding form, as it is in the blessed in heaven. Rather, it occurs through a passing impression, as when a person turns white with fright for only a moment.[48] So prophets do not always prophesy; neither do they see God in God's essence. But a prophet is changed by her experience, and she is rendered more capable of receiving prophecies in the future. While the knowledge itself is transient and momentary, the prophet can be shaped by the experience. The "habitlike" sense of prophetic knowledge comes forth more clearly in the Latin than in the English translation, since "*habilitas*" translates as "aptitude."[49] For Thomas, prophecy can never be a "*habitus*," or a habit, but it can provide a certain "*habilitas*," or an aptitude for receiving prophecies. It can render the prophet more apt to become enlightened by divine light in the future. One can sense Thomas struggling here to capture at one and the same time the possibility that receiving prophecies affects the person receiving them and that this does not happen in such a way that the knowledge becomes habitual rather than transitory.

Thomas orders the various instances of prophecy into a flexible framework. Prophetic knowledge can be imparted in two main ways.

In the first, the prophet does not enjoy an infused vision, but rather she is enlightened in order to judge something that is known through natural reason, as in the case of Solomon. The second way includes an infused vision that informs the intellect and terminates in an act of judgment. The nature of the forms changes the way the prophetic knowledge is received; each one deepens the prophetic light at work. If the form is corporeal, the prophet's external senses are stimulated. Her mind is not abstracted from her senses when something is presented to her by means of sensible form. Sometimes these are divinely formed for a special purpose, like the burning bush shown to Moses (Ex. 3:2) or the writing shown to Daniel on Belshazzar's wall (Dan. 5). At other times, an object is ordained by divine providence to signify something else, as when Noah's ark was meant to signify the Church. In all of these cases the person witnesses the image *through* her sensible organs, not in spite of them.

But when prophetic revelation is conveyed by images to the imagination, abstraction from the senses is needed. This abstraction prevents the things seen in the imagination to be mistaken for objects received through one's external senses. The abstraction occurs without subverting the order of nature and with a well-ordered cause. This is an important claim for Thomas, because this distinguishes prophets from those who are possessed or out of their senses due to mental illness.[50] There are two different ways that imaginary forms are given to the prophet. In the first way, God impresses an image on her that she has never encountered before, as when someone born blind has infused into her imagination colorful images. Another way is that images that already exist in a person's mind are rearranged or ordered in such a manner as to provide the vehicle for the prophecy. Jeremiah's vision of the boiling pot (Jer. 1:13), for example, was not a new image he had never seen before. Instead, God draws the image from Jeremiah's memory and arranges it in his imagination in order to symbolize impending danger.[51] If the form arises in the imagination, God produces a sensible phantasm in the imagination either immediately or by rearranging images from the prophet's memory. If the form is a purely intellectual vision without assistance from the imagination, God infuses the intelligible form directly into the intellect. According to the order of knowing, a pure intellectual vision that does not involve imaginary forms is more perfect than one that does, for the cognoscitive act depends directly on God. Thomas admits, however, that prophecies that involve imaginative forms enjoy a certain pride of place, since the knowledge received in prophecy most often engages the imagination.[52] To summarize: The weakest form of prophetic knowledge includes not an infused vision but only a certain enlightenment to help the prophet judge something known through natural reason. When prophetic knowledge involves an infused vision, it can come in a corporeal, imaginative, or intellectual form, with the intellectual being the strongest form of prophecy. Prophetic knowledge, then, spans a wide range of possibilities, both concerning subject matter and with respect to method of delivery.

The strength of prophecy is even affected by the context within which the prophecy occurs. The grade of prophecy that occurs when one is awake is more perfect than one that occurs in a dream since one's capacity to understand is stronger when one is awake than when one is sleeping. The grade of prophecy is also higher when the one who speaks is seen than when one only hears the words, whether this is in a dream or in a vision. It is also higher when the one who speaks is seen in the image of an angel rather than that of a human being, and highest, of course, if it is seen in the image of God.[53] Thomas's treatment of prophecy casts a very large net to catch disparate instances of scriptural prophecies. He provides in his systematic works a taxonomy of prophecy that brings these differing instances into a cohesive whole.

While we have seen that prophetic knowledge comes in various ways, its two main features are reception (*acceptio*) and judgment (*judicium*), although judgment is its absolutely key feature. The teaching analogy falls short here, as God enlightens the prophet inwardly in a way that a teacher could never do to a student. We can tell that judgment is the key feature of prophetic knowledge because someone can be called a prophet even if his intellect is enlightened for the purpose of judging things seen in the imagination by others, as happened when Joseph interpreted Pharaoh's dream.[54] Supernatural judgment is given to the prophet through the light infused into her, which gives her strength to judge.[55] The central element is the judgment of what is received through the senses. That the reception of images is secondary can be seen in the case of Pharaoh, who is not properly called a prophet, even if he was the one who received the dream. A proper prophecy entails either a judgment of images received by another (as occurs when Joseph interprets Pharaoh's dreams) or a reception of images in one's own imagination that terminate in the act of judgment.

Thomas's conviction that judgment is the central feature of prophetic knowledge was strengthened over the course of his corpus. He inherited and drew from an understanding of prophecy held by Augustine,[56] whose neo-Platonic epistemology led him to accentuate the reception of the vision over the act of judgment. For Augustine, the greater the divine illuminating light, the greater the prophecy at work. But since Thomas generally worked within an Aristotelian epistemology, he saw knowledge principally as an act in which the act of judgment plays an essential role.[57]

This development took place between his writing of the *Commentary on Isaiah* (1252–53) and that of the *Secunda secundae* of the *ST* (1268–71).[58] In the Isaiah commentary we learn that prophecy consists in knowledge of things that are far from human knowing and includes a corporeal, imaginative, or intellectual vision.[59] Its fundamental element, however, is the intellectual vision, whose role is not yet clearly defined. Thomas does affirm in this text that the prophetic knowledge that emerges from the intellectual vision is called "prophecy" in its most proper sense and that the other two forms of vision (corporeal and imaginative) are called "prophecy" by participation. But he has yet to reflect on the role of reception (*acceptio*) and judgment (*judicium*) in the prophetic experience. In later works, Thomas would progressively distance himself from Augustine's understanding of the cognoscitive process in prophecy. While he would maintain the term "intellectual vision" for the reception (*acceptio*) of the intellectual form in the mind, he would be much more careful in making the distinction between this reception and the rational act of judgment.[60] By the time he wrote the *DVer*, he stipulated that what is really constitutive of prophecy is the *judicium* and that this corresponds in large part to what had been called "intellectual vision."[61] The advance between the *Commentary on Isaiah* (1247) and the *DVer* (1256) is noteworthy. Prophecy is now definitely seen as an act and not a habit. It has been disentangled from the rigid definition of the vision of future contingents and now covers a broad range of possible topics. Finally, the "intellectual vision" from the *Commentary on Isaiah* has been expanded and now refers primarily to the act of judgment.[62]

Prophecy changed with the advent of history, and it can be categorized in three epochs: before the law, under the law, and under grace. Before the law, Abraham and the other patriarchs were taught things pertinent to faith in God. Under the law, prophecies pertinent to faith in God were made in a stronger way since not only certain special persons or families but whole peoples were instructed in these matters. Moses, for example, was more fully instructed in the simplicity of the divine essence than were the patriarchs. In the time of grace, the Son of God Himself revealed the mystery of the Trinity.[63]

With respect to the guidance of human acts, however, the prophetic revelations do not vary according to the course of time but rather as the individual circumstances require.[64] At all times, people were divinely instructed about what they were to do according to what was needed for the spiritual welfare (*ad salutem*) of the elect.[65] Thomas even documents postresurrection prophets. These include Agabus and the four maidens, the daughters of Philip from the Acts of the Apostles, and an early church figure named John. Citing Augustine, Thomas affirms that even the fourth-century emperor Theodosius sent for the prophet John. This prophet assured Theodosius of certain victory against Maximus.[66] We can see that Thomas himself documents post-resurrection prophets, both those who are named within the scriptural texts and at least one who lived during the growth of the fourth century Christian community.

Thomas was working from within an Aristotelian epistemology in his treatment of prophecy, even as he wedded this to a neo-Platonic cosmology. Nowhere is this more apparent than in his discussion of the role of angels in prophetic knowledge. He writes that while prophecy is ultimately due to the work of a divine light, angels serve an indispensable role as mediators between the incommensurability of God's way of knowing and the limited nature of human knowing. While God has chosen the one to whom He wants to impart prophetic messages throughout history, He deploys angels in particular as divine instruments of prophecy. Charity, which makes the human person a friend of God, is a perfection of the will; God alone can bring this about.[67] But in prophecies, angels can serve as intermediaries between God and the human person. Angels play a mediating role here because prophecy is a perfection of the intellect, not a perfection of the will. God is the primary source of the prophetic light itself, by which the mind of the prophet is enlightened. But an angelic light can strengthen and prepare the prophet to receive the divine light. Since the power of the divine light is most simple and most universal, there is no proportion between the divine light and the reception of this light by the human person in this life. The angelic mind is more commensurate with the human mind, so union with an angelic light can limit and specify the divine light and enable it to be received by the human person. This is part of the work proper to angels. The formation of the species in the imaginative power must be attributed properly to the angels, since the whole of bodily creation is under the direction of spiritual creation. The formation of species in the imaginative power uses a bodily organ that angels can direct and shape.[68]

We have seen how there are as many ways of receiving a prophecy as there are ways of receiving knowledge. Thomas stretched his treatment of prophecy to account for very different scriptural examples of the phenomenon, for he was sensitive to variations within the history of salvation. Prophecies can simply involve an external image or they can engage the imagination. Sometimes, even, they involve only the strengthening of an intellectual light. The key feature of prophetic knowledge is the act of judgment, although most prophecies also include the reception of an image. Throughout salvation history, prophecies have changed according to a particular community's needs. After the death of Christ, prophecies have emerged on a strictly ad hoc basis in order to direct different communities' behaviors, the summit of which is divine worship.

Prophecy 301: The Prophetic Student

Who is chosen for prophecy? Thomas insists that after the coming of Christ, prophets can still emerge in the Church: "At all times there have not been lacking persons having the spirit of prophecy, not indeed for the declaration of any new doctrine of faith, but for the direction of human acts."[69] So prophets are not relegated to scriptural history long gone. Instead, prophecy is a permanent element in Church life. No natural disposition is required, but some dispositions more than others can hinder the reception of prophecies.[70] While anyone could be chosen to prophesy, living an evil life—as would stand to reason—provides a hindrance to prophecy. In addition, strong passions and an unmeasured pursuit of external things inhibit a person from contemplating spiritual things.[71] Prophecy pertains to the intellect, whose act precedes the will. A person, then, who lacks charity or sanctifying grace can receive a prophetic revelation. In a technical sense, an evil person can receive the gift of prophecy. Although prophecy is a gift of the Holy Spirit, the Holy Spirit is given not with the gift of prophecy but only with the gift of charity.[72] In other words, the Holy Spirit moves the prophet inwardly for the sake of others without taking root in her in order to sanctify her. We will see in the next chapter that Thomas takes this very seriously when interpreting the words of Scripture. The person receiving the prophecy can even choose to misuse or ignore it. Jonah, for example, reacts to God's message by running away rather than by going to Nineveh and preaching (Jonah 1:1–3).[73] Properly and simply, prophecy is conveyed by divine revelation alone, yet the revelation that is given by demons may be called prophecy only in a limited sense.[74] The Holy Spirit can even speak through false prophets, for "God makes use even of the wicked for the profit of the good."[75] In bearing witness to the truth, God's foes unwittingly make the truth more credible.[76] Even those who pronounced oracles in ancient Greece, the Sibyls, can transmit prophecy. *Anyone* whom God chooses as an instrument to deliver a message to the community of faith can become a prophet.

The gift of the discernment of spirits is intimately linked to the gift of prophecy. Some things done by evil spirits are similar to the things whereby faith is confirmed, both in the working of miracles and in the revelation of future events. In order for us to distinguish true spirits from false, the help of divine grace is needed.[77] Discernment of spirits, then, has a crucial role to play in the prophetic process.

While nothing false can come under prophecy, discerning the prophetic from the human elements in any given utterance is no simple matter. The prophet does not always know what she prophesies. For example, as we will see in the next chapter, Caiaphas and the soldiers who divided Christ's garments prophesied without knowing what they were saying and doing.[78] When the person knows that she is being moved by the Holy Spirit to think, say, or do something, she is properly a prophet. But when she is moved without knowing it, this is not perfect prophecy but instead a "prophetic instinct." In this case, the person is not able to fully distinguish whether her thoughts are conceived by divine instinct or by her own spirit. A prophetic certitude is lacking here, and this instinct is something imperfect in the genus of prophecy.[79] However, since the prophet's mind is a deficient instrument, even true prophets do not know all that the Holy Spirit means by the things they see, speak, or do. Since prophecy is a transient passion and not a form of habitual knowledge, one and the same prophet can receive various degrees of prophetic revelation at different times.[80] Sometimes prophecy is conferred on one who seems least disposed to it, someone one would *least* expect to have it; this is done so we can readily attribute the prophecy to divine power.[81] Scripture itself invites us to conclude that prophets need not be believers in Jesus. "Prophecy" is applied to them in a relative and limited sense, but Scripture already documents this complex phenomenon. We will see how seriously Thomas takes these scriptural texts in the next chapter.

We have examined how Thomas took disparate data from Scripture and developed a complex and subtle account of prophecy that is both flexible and cohesive. The main operative metaphor here is that of teaching; there are as many pedagogies as specific teaching contexts require. Sometimes a prophet's intellectual light is strengthened so he can know something that can be known by natural reason. At other times, prophecies come in corporeal, imaginative, or intellectual form so that the prophet can come to know something beyond the bounds of human reason. The central feature of a prophetic experience is the act of judgment since prophecy properly speaking is an act of the intellect: The prophet (generally) receives images and judges them to be true. Each instance of prophetic revelation falls within the larger pattern of God's desire to manifest Himself in all of creation. Prophecy is just one particular set of ways in which this manifestation takes shape, and it always serves the wider faith community. Ultimately, though, prophetic knowledge is partial, incomplete, and mixed with darkness. It will give way to the clarity of vision at the end of time.

In the next chapter we turn to particular prophetic figures from Scripture about whom Thomas comments, in order to put his taxonomy to work. We will then take up the question of how Muhammad might figure in this taxonomy and how he might relate to this cast of characters.

CHAPTER FOUR

Scriptural Prophets
and Muhammad

The next step toward paving the way for our examination of Muhammad is to turn toward scriptural figures whom Thomas Aquinas highlights as prophets. Here again, the temptation is to draw parallels too quickly. Thomas's analysis of these scriptural figures begins to open up the space necessary to entertain the possibility of Muhammad's prophethood.

We have seen that a consistent theme emerges in the taxonomy of prophecy that Thomas builds in his systematic works: God chooses whom God wants to be prophets. There is no job description. There is no way to turn oneself into a prophet by one's own abilities. Sometimes God chooses a particularly unlikely figure in order to place in greater relief the divine power at work in that person. The two main features of prophecy are a reception of images—be they corporeal, imaginative, or intellectual—and their termination in the act of judgment. Thomas explicitly makes room for postresurrection prophets who have roles to play until the end of time—particularly roles to direct the acts of the believing community. These acts culminate in divine worship. Prophets serve the faith community, the *viatores*, with partial, enigmatic, and piecemeal knowledge until the end of time, where knowledge by faith, under which prophetic knowledge operates, will give way, as will our anticipation in theological hope. Only charity will remain.

This chapter turns explicitly to Thomas's scriptural commentaries and his reflection on some unlikely prophets—even some figures who reject Jesus and yet speak and act prophetically. It then turns back to the taxonomy from chapter 3 in order to draw some conclusions about these figures. Finally, it recalls our reading in chapter 2 of Vatican II documents on non-Christians generally and Muslims in particular, where Christians and Muslims share an overlapping web of beliefs, and draws some preliminary conclusions about the role of Muhammad in this taxonomy of prophecy.

We now turn to an analysis of what Thomas writes in his scriptural commentaries about several unlikely prophets. Some figures participate in prophecy by speaking (Caiaphas, Balaam, and his donkey) and acting (the Roman soldiers at the crucifixion), without understanding the significance of what they are doing. Another's intellect is strengthened in order to understand things known by natural reason (Solomon). And a final one participated in prophetic knowledge as a wayfarer (Jesus). Each of these examples helps to set up border cases in the prophetic experience. At one edge, there is an animal, Balaam's donkey, which could hardly have been said to "know" what it was saying. At the directly opposite edge stands Jesus, who was fully human and fully divine, who knew by beatific knowing and is still called a prophet. Solomon stands at yet another edge, since his prophecy did not concern things of God; rather, only his human reason was strengthened. Balaam stands at another edge, as he was an evil person, a diviner, and yet God put him to prophetic use. Caiaphas and the Roman soldiers are also found at an edge, since they did not know what they were saying (in the case of Caiaphas) or doing (in the case of the Roman soldiers). These individual instances of prophecy embody the theoretical framework outlined in the previous chapter. At the end of this analysis, we will be able to draw some preliminary conclusions that invite a theoretical openness to Muhammad's participation in the prophetic process.

CAIAPHAS

Caiaphas offers our most robust example of someone speaking prophetically who did not believe in Jesus; he was, in fact, the high priest responsible for sending Jesus to his death. Thomas's most extensive treatment of Caiaphas is found in chapter 11 of his *Commentary on the Gospel of John*, in *In Io*. In his scriptural commentaries Thomas leads the reader through the fruits of the medieval practice of *lectio divina*, in which meditation on the words of Scripture introduce readers to worlds of meaning not initially apparent on the sacred page.

Chapter 11 of the Gospel begins just after Jesus had raised Lazarus from the dead. Many of the Jews who went with Martha and Mary to the tomb began to believe in Jesus. Some of them returned to the Pharisees and told them what he had done. By way of response, the chief priests and the Pharisees called a meeting of the council to discuss the ramifications of Jesus's miracle work. Some of them were concerned that if they let Jesus continue to perform signs, everyone would believe in him. The Romans' fear of a Jewish revolt, in turn, would lead to the destruction of both the Jewish temple and the nation. The passage in the chapter that is relevant to our discussion reads:

> [49] But one of them, Caiaphas, who was high priest that year, said to them, "You know nothing at all!
> [50] You do not understand that it is better for you to have one man die for the people than to have the whole nation destroyed."
> [51] He did not say this on his own, but being high priest that year he prophesied that Jesus was about to die for the nation,
> [52] and not for the nation only, but to gather into one the dispersed children of God.
> [53] So from that day on they planned to put him to death.[1]

Thomas first entertains the possibility that the Jews could have gone to the chief priests to tell them about Jesus in order to soften them toward Jesus and to reproach them for conspiring against him. But he then suggests a more plausible reading of this passage. The Jews went to the chief priests to incite them against Jesus, "for they were unbelievers and were scandalized at the miracle."[2] These are the ones about whom, in chapter 12 of the same Gospel, we read, "Although he had performed so many signs in their presence, they did not believe in him . . . for they loved human glory more than the glory that comes from God."[3]

The Jews who witnessed the raising of Lazarus were not the only ones affected. Their leaders—the chief priests in charge of sacred matters and the Pharisees who had the "appearance" (*speciem*) of religion—were also implicated. Thomas comments that this led to the fulfillment of Genesis 49:5 ("Simeon and Levi are brothers; weapons of violence are their swords"). The chief priests descended from the tribe of Levi and the Pharisees from Simeon. The reader understands that their wickedness was deliberate, since they "gathered the council [*concilio*]" in order to make their plans. Medieval readers who could recall scriptural passages from memory would join Thomas in recognizing in the word "council" echoes from Genesis 49:6 ("May I never come into their council") and Psalm 1:1 ("Happy are those who do not follow the advice [*consilium*] of the wicked"). But they would also recall Proverbs 21:30 ("No wisdom, no understanding, no counsel [*consilium*], can avail against the Lord"). The word "council" is pregnant with meaning for medieval listeners. Thomas finds in that word both the guilt of the high priests and the ultimate vindication of Christ. This word provides the theme of the whole passage. While the council of Jewish leaders condemned Jesus to death, in the end no "counsel" availed against the Lord, since the death of Jesus of Nazareth led to the ultimate vindication of sin and the possibility of resurrection for the human race.

The chief priests did not know what to do about the man who performed many signs. Thomas comments that they were so blind that they continued to call him a "man," even after Jesus had demonstrated his divinity. And while they recognized that this man "performs many signs," their wickedness blinded them to their meaning. They were, in fact, blind to their own words. At root, they feared the losses that would follow from letting Jesus perform signs. They were worried about losing their spiritual leadership because they knew that faith in Jesus would mean a loss of faith in the leaders who persecuted Him. They also feared that the Romans would destroy their temple and ultimately their nation. The Romans had ordered that only they be allowed to appoint a king over the Jews. The leaders were afraid that if the Romans heard that they were regarding Christ as king, they would look on the Jews as rebels.[4]

Now Caiaphas sets out to resolve the problem of what to do about Jesus. The Evangelist calls the one making the decision by his name and his office. His name, "Caiaphas," was "appropriate to his wicked-ness" ("*convenit suae malitiae*") because in etymological terms the name means "investigator," attesting to his presumption, "sagacious," testifying to his cunning, and "vomiting," pointing to his foolishness. His office of high priest also describes who he is. In Leviticus 8, the Lord appoints one high priest, at whose death another was to succeed him. But Thomas notes that as ambitions and quarrels grew among the Jews, it was agreed that there should be a number of high priests. He hints here that the office of high priest had become degraded, even by selling the office for money. Thomas concludes, then, that the Gospel already signals the depravity of the person set to solve the problem of Jesus simply by reference to his name and office.

Next, the Evangelist provides the words of the one making the de-cision. He reproaches the Jews for their sluggishness ("*ignaviam*") when he tells them that they know nothing at all and that they do not understand the meaning of the situation at hand. Caiaphas then reveals his wickedness in claiming that "it is expedient for you that one man should die for the people." This is the key passage of the selected text, and Thomas spends some time unpacking its meaning.

These words have a double meaning, one according to the inten-tion of Caiaphas and another according to the explanation of the Evan-gelist. In modern terms, we would call this dramatic irony. In saying these words, Caiaphas thought he was fulfilling Deuteronomy 13:1, where the Lord had commanded, "If a prophet arises among you, or a dreamer of dreams, and if he says, 'Let us go after other gods,' that prophet or that dreamer of dreams shall be put to death."[5] Caiaphas believed that Jesus would turn people away from the true worship of God and was therefore a candidate for death under the Deuteronomic law. He was convinced that one man should be scorned (*contemnere*) for the public good (*communi republica*).

But the Evangelist offers another meaning of these words when he says, "He did not say this of his own accord." The Evangelist rejects that Caiaphas spoke of his own impulse (*instinctu proprio*). When some-one speaks of his own reason, he speaks of his own accord. But when he is moved to speak under a "higher" and "external impulse" he no longer speaks of his own accord.[6] In general, this can happen in two ways. Sometimes a person is moved by the divine Spirit, as in Matthew

10:20, when Jesus sends out his twelve disciples to evangelize and assures them that "it is not you who speak, but the Spirit of your Father
speaking through you." A wrinkle arises here: A wicked spirit can also
move one to speak or act, as in the case of "those who rave" (*sicut ar-
reptitii*). In both of these cases, a person can be said to prophesy. Remember that God can use even evil spirits in the prophetic process.
Thomas notes that sometimes a person may speak by the impulse of
the Holy Spirit or of an evil spirit in such a way that the person loses
the use of her reason and is somehow seized. At other times, the use of
reason remains. When the senses are overflowing due to a divine impression, the reason is hindered, disturbed, and seized. But an evil
spirit can also unite itself to the physical organ of the imagination, hin-
dering the person's use of reason. And yet the person under the influence of the evil spirit is never forced to consent.

The question naturally arises: Did Caiaphas speak by the impulse
of a holy spirit or an evil one? It seems at first blush that an evil spirit
impelled him to speak, for the Holy Spirit is the spirit of truth; the
wicked spirit, naturally, is the spirit of falsehood. And it is obvious that
Caiaphas spoke a lie when he said, "It is expedient for you that one man
should die." It seems that a raving wicked spirit impelled him to speak
such a lie. While this is the surface reading of the words in this text,
Thomas probes their deeper meaning. He suggests that the first reading
does not agree with the words of the Evangelist because he would not
have added "who was high priest that year." The Evangelist "mentions
the dignity of Caiaphas in order to suggest that he spoke by an impulse of the Holy Spirit to speak truths about the future for the precise
benefit of their subjects."[7] So the claim "it is expedient for you that one
man should die for the people" turns out to be true, but not in the sense
that Caiaphas intended. The death of Christ considered in itself was expedient for all, even for those who killed Him, since Christ had come to
save all, but especially those who believe in Him (1 Tim. 4:10).

Given what Thomas had previously written in this commentary
about the etymological root of Caiaphas's name and the degradation
of his office, one would not have expected him to claim prophecy in
this instance. But Thomas takes the Evangelist so seriously that he cannot ignore the words on the page. The Gospel writer indicates in no

uncertain terms that Caiaphas "prophesied." A reader of this passage would logically conclude that if a person prophesies, then she must be a prophet. But Thomas appeals to Origen in signaling that this conclusion is faulty. If one is a prophet, one prophesies. But it does not follow that everyone who prophesies is a prophet. There has to be something more to the office of "prophet" than simply the act of prophesying. For not everyone who does something just is just, but one who is just does just things.[8] We conclude, then, that while Caiaphas did prophesy, he did not necessarily benefit from the full office of prophet. The office of high priest had been degraded by the time of Caiaphas, and yet the Evangelist still holds it in esteem. However, the office of prophet he reserves for those truly deserving of the name, even if the "high priest" Caiaphas is said properly to have prophesied. We have uncovered the first layer of the scriptural passage by distinguishing between an act of prophecy and the office of prophet.

But Thomas does not stop here. He uncovers the next layer. Prophecy includes an act of seeing and an act of announcing. Sometimes, though, a person does both—speaking and announcing—and yet is not, properly speaking, a prophet. As examples, Nebuchadnezzar and Pharaoh each had a prophetic vision and announced it to others. But they lacked the crucial ingredient of prophecy: the understanding of the vision. Caiaphas, while he did not have a prophetic vision, did speak in a prophetic manner when he announced Christ's death. Sometimes the Holy Spirit moves one to all that pertains to prophecy and sometimes to only one thing. In the case of Caiaphas, the Holy Spirit enlightened neither his mind nor his imagination. Consequently, his mind and imagination remained intent on evil. However, the Holy Spirit moved his tongue to tell the manner in which the salvation of the people was to be accomplished. Thomas concludes, "Thus, he is not called a prophet except insofar as he performed a prophetic act in announcing, his imagination and reason remaining fixed in the contrary."[9] But in the last sentence of this part of the commentary, he comes to the surprising conclusion that Caiaphas cannot be considered a prophet any more than Balaam's donkey could be. Given the reasoning that precedes this concluding sentence, we should take it to mean that he is speaking here of the office of prophet rather than the act of prophecy. Caiaphas did not benefit from the office of prophet, but he did participate in the act of prophecy. This is no denial of the argument he had just put forth about Caiaphas exhibiting a characteristic of prophecy. It underlines, rather, the distinction between acting prophetically as a partial participation in the prophetic experience and enjoying the full office of prophet. We will see how this reading of the last sentence is bolstered by Thomas's reflections in his other scriptural commentaries. The question of what kind of person could enjoy the full office of prophet had not yet been fully addressed in his corpus, as this commentary was one of his earliest works, dating from 1256.

The other scriptural commentaries that take up this issue do not offer the extended treatment of Caiaphas offered by the *Commentary on John*, but they do add some crucial details to our discussion. In his *Commentary on Hebrews* (*Super Heb.*) 11:32–35, Thomas asks whether those listed in this scriptural passage were all prophets.[10] He answers that the Holy Spirit can move one to do three things: to know, to speak, and to do. This movement occurs in two ways, either with the act of understanding or without it. Sometimes, the Holy Spirit moves the prophet by making him understand what is seen, as in the case of Isaiah and the other prophets. Such a person is called a "seer." Other times, though, a person receives a vision without understanding it, as in the case of Pharaoh's dream or Belshazzar's vision. But these cannot properly be called prophets because they lacked the understanding of their visions, which is necessary for prophecy.

The Holy Spirit also moves one to speak in two ways: sometimes he knows what he says, as in the case of David, or, on other occasions, he speaks without knowing, as in the case of Caiaphas and perhaps (*forte*) Balaam. When someone is moved to do something, the person might know what he is doing, such as when Jeremiah hid his girdle by the Euphrates, but perhaps the person does not know what he is doing, such as when the soldiers divided Jesus's garments. The soldiers knew nothing of the mystery to which that division was ordained. Thomas concludes: "Therefore, it pertains to the notion of a prophet that he know what he sees or says or does. This is the way John says that Caiaphas prophesied, because he had something characteristic of prophecy. This movement of the Holy Spirit is called an instinct by

Augustine."[11] Caiaphas enjoyed something characteristic of prophecy, even if he did not enjoy the full office of prophet, given that he did not understand the true meaning of his words. We can see Thomas taking the Evangelist's words seriously. Thomas recognizes that if the Gospel writer claimed that Caiaphas prophesied, he must in some sense be a prophet, even if he does not enjoy the full benefits of the office. This partial expression of the full account of prophecy he terms "prophetic instinct," drawing on Augustine. It could be that Thomas's insistence on the key role of the act of judgment in prophecy makes it more difficult for him to appreciate Caiaphas's prophecy than Augustine's earlier account of prophecy, where the accent was placed on "intellectual vision." And yet Thomas wants to accept the words of the Evangelist. While he recognizes the words of the Gospel that Caiaphas prophesied, he clearly stops short of granting the title of prophet to Caiaphas. Caiaphas enjoyed something that characterizes prophecy, but he cannot be called a prophet in the fullest sense of the term. In the *Commentary on Hebrews*, Thomas adopts Augustine's term "instinct" in relationship to prophecy. But the distinction between *acceptio* and *judicium* that emerged in the later *Secunda secundae* of the *ST* had not yet taken shape in Thomas's thought. As a result, we have here an acknowledgement of Caiaphas's participation in the experience of prophecy without a full account of how it takes place.

Thomas's *Commentary on Corinthians* (*Super I Cor.*) offers us another distinction to help us understand Caiaphas's relationship to prophetic knowledge. Thomas comments on 1 Cor. 12:3: "Therefore I want you to understand that no one speaking by the Spirit of God ever says 'Let Jesus be cursed!' and no one can say 'Jesus is Lord' except by the Holy Spirit." Not everyone who says "Lord Jesus" says it in the Holy Spirit. Someone could proclaim the title "Lord Jesus" but do so in such a way that it does not come from an interior movement of the Holy Spirit. One could pronounce the title ironically, or even out of spite. Saying something in the Holy Spirit can be understood in two ways. In the first way, the Holy Spirit moves but does not possess the person. The Holy Spirit can move the hearts (*corda*) of certain people to speak while not dwelling in them. This is, in fact, the work of gratuitous grace, a grace given for the good of others but not transformative of itself to the person who receives it. When Caiaphas predicted the utility of Jesus's death, he did not speak from himself but was moved by the Holy Spirit for the good of others. Caiaphas himself did not come to possess the Holy Spirit in the prophetic experience. This means that no one can say anything true unless moved by the Holy Spirit, who is the spirit of truth, as is said in John 16:13: "When the Spirit of truth comes, he will guide you into all the truth."[12] We find here that the Holy Spirit can move the hearts of certain people to speak while not dwelling in them. Caiaphas, then, was properly moved by the Holy Spirit when he spoke prophetically, but the Holy Spirit did not dwell in him. What difference does this make? Caiaphas spoke prophetically without being sanctified in the process. This is, of course, how a gratuitous grace works, and Thomas will come to classify prophecy as a gratuitous grace.

If we take these three scriptural commentaries collectively, we recognize that Thomas was uncomfortable with assigning the full office of prophet to Caiaphas. But he had to take the words of the Evangelist seriously. While he did not yet have fully in place the later distinctions that we find in the systematic works and had not yet clearly nailed down the epistemology of prophetic knowledge, he did recognize that Caiaphas participated in the prophetic experience. The later assignation of prophecy as a gratuitous grace whose key feature is judgment was not yet in place as he was writing these scriptural commentaries. Caiaphas's heart was moved to speak the truth even though the Holy Spirit did not dwell in him and he did not understand what he was saying. His mind was still darkened and intent upon evil. But lest we conclude that Thomas changed his mind about Caiaphas later in his career, when he had had the opportunity to hammer out the epistemology of the prophetic process, we should note that in the *Secunda pars* of the *ST*, he affirms in no less than the *sed contra* of an article that not all prophets know what they prophesy, since Caiaphas prophesied and yet did not know what he was saying.[13] While Caiaphas did not enjoy the full benefits of prophecy, the Holy Spirit spoke through him without dwelling in him. In the scriptural commentaries, Thomas does not yet have the epistemological distinctions of *acceptio* and *judicium* laid out, but he does begin to offer some preliminary distinctions. Caiaphas could be said to have enjoyed a "prophetic instinct" though he could not clearly distinguish between what was of God and what was of an evil spirit. He received some of the benefits of prophecy and put them to ill use by condemning Jesus to death, although ironically it was this act that ultimately led to God's offer of universal salvation on the cross. Caiaphas offers us the quintessential example of the character we would least expect to be called upon to prophesy. Scripture signals this fact, and Thomas affirms it.

THE ROMAN SOLDIERS

Thomas spends less time reflecting on the Roman soldiers than he does reflecting on Caiaphas, as Caiaphas is a much more perplexing scriptural figure than they are. These soldiers acted as pawns in a wider political conspiracy against Jesus. Thomas suspects that the same pattern was at work with the soldiers as with Caiaphas, except that this time prophecy took the form of gestures instead of words.

In the *ST*, Thomas joins the example of the Roman soldiers, who did not understand the meaning of what they were doing with Jesus's garments, to that of Caiaphas, who lacked understanding of the prophetic words spoken by his tongue. The Holy Spirit moved each to act or speak, but not in a way that belongs to the proper meaning of prophecy. In the case of the soldiers and Caiaphas, we are dealing not with perfect prophecy but with a prophetic instinct (*non est perfecta prophetia, sed quidam instinctus propheticus*).[14] Thomas incorporates the same reasoning when he adds the Roman soldiers to the example of Caiaphas already examined above in discussing the *Commentary on Hebrews*: both enjoyed a prophetic instinct rather than expressing prophecy in the fullest sense of the term.

What the Roman soldiers add to our discussion, then, is simply an amplification of what prophecy means. It need not include words but could instead involve an act that fulfills a prophecy. In this case, the Roman soldiers fulfilled Psalm 22:18, where David foreshadows the way Christ would die when he complains, "They divide my clothes among themselves, and for my clothing they cast lots." And yet the soldiers failed to understand the meaning of what they were doing. According to a Christian gloss on a Hebrew text, they were pathetically casting lots for Jesus's garments, while David had originally been directly condemning Christ's death. But Thomas understood that God can take even the seemingly meaningless act of gambling for a convicted criminal's garments and turn it into the fulfillment of a prophecy.

BALAAM'S DONKEY

While Balaam's donkey emerges in Thomas's corpus in only a handful of instances, this example continues to illustrate our argument that God uses whomever He chooses to communicate to humanity, but here with some scriptural humor. Sometimes this even means the admittedly unusual instance of speaking through a donkey. The story in Numbers 22:21–35 relates how Balaam was traveling with two servants to meet with Balak, king of Moab, when an angel of the Lord with a sword in his hand stood in his way along the road. The donkey caught sight of the angel, while Balaam failed to see him. Instead of heeding Balaam's command to continue on the path, the donkey bolted into a vineyard. Balaam responded by striking the donkey as a way of forcing him back onto the path. The donkey responded by crushing Balaam's foot against a wall. For this, the donkey received another lashing. The angel came closer to the donkey and his master, so that the donkey had nowhere to move, and it collapsed under Balaam, who responded, for a third time, with a thrashing. The Lord then opened the mouth of the donkey, who reminded Balaam of his steadfast loyalty. It was only then that the master's eyes were opened—intellectually, spiritually, and physically—and he saw the angel of the Lord.

Balaam's donkey is mentioned in a few places in Thomas's corpus in relation to the issue of prophecy. In a question in the *ST* concerning whether the first temptation of Christ by Satan in the form of a serpent was fitting, an objector writes that the serpent is an irrational animal. Wisdom, speech, and punishment do not befit an irrational animal. The serpent, then, is unfittingly described in Genesis 3:1 as "more crafty than any other wild animal that the Lord God had made," and it is unfittingly stated to have spoken to the woman Eve and to have been punished by God. Thomas responds by citing Augustine,[15] who wrote that the serpent is the most prudent or subtle on account of the cunning of the devil that wrought his wiles in it. When we speak of a prudent or cunning tongue, we mean that it is the instrument of a prudent or cunning person. This person says something in this particular case that is prudent or cunning. The serpent did not understand the sounds that were conveyed through it to the woman, nor was its soul changed to possess a rational nature, since not even human beings, who are rational by nature, know what they say when a demon speaks in them. So the serpent spoke to the human person "even as the ass on which Balaam sat spoke to him, except that the former was the work of a devil, whereas the latter was the work of an angel."[16] An angel spoke through Balaam's donkey—this certainly sounds as if it fits the characteristics of how Thomas has defined prophetic speech.

Balaam's donkey is also brought into an argument concerning whether demons can cooperate in the working of miracles in the *De Potentia.* Answering an objection, Thomas writes that a demon cannot give a dog the power of speech miraculously as when it is given to the dumb, but rather by some kind of local movement the dog makes sounds to be heard like words composed of letters and syllables: "It is thus that we may understand Balaam's ass to have spoken, although in this case it was by the action of a good angel."[17] Here again, Thomas recognizes that an angel spoke through Balaam's donkey.

We have already seen in a previous section that Thomas ends his reflection about Caiaphas in the *Commentary on the Gospel of John* by stating that he is no more a prophet than Balaam's donkey. We can now add that the angel of the Lord spoke through Balaam's donkey. While certainly we would not expect a donkey to participate in prophecy in the full sense of the term, we note here that Scripture attests to the fact that an angel moved a particular donkey to speak prophetically. Donkeys were used as a regular means of transportation in the scriptural landscape, so this humorous example, while foreign to a modern ear, would certainly have been familiar to the original listeners, and even to Thomas's medieval confreres. Thomas incorporates this scriptural scene in his discussion of prophecy. This reinforces the notion that God chooses whom He wills to participate in the prophetic experience, even a creature as strikingly unusual as a donkey.

BALAAM

In the passage from the *Commentary on Corinthians* that we discussed in relation to Caiaphas, Thomas includes Balaam as an example of someone who was moved by the Holy Spirit to predict many true things without being "possessed" by the Holy Spirit. Balaam's predictions came true. Although the book of Numbers (chaps. 23 and 24) attests to the fact that he was moved by the Holy Spirit, he was not possessed by the Holy Spirit. It is possible to say something while being both moved and possessed by the Holy Spirit. In this case, the person speaks from both heart (*corde*) and deed (*opere*), as when a believer says "Jesus is Lord" and both reveres and obeys Him.[18] Here again, we find the distinction between being moved by the Holy Spirit to speak and being possessed by the Holy Spirit.

In a passage in the *DVer* where Thomas discusses the difference between the act of reception and the act of judgment in any given prophecy, he mentions Balaam as one who received prophecy. In the matter of judgment, the cognition of one who is awake is preferable to that of one who is asleep. The judgment of the person who is awake is free, while the judgment of the sleeping person is encumbered. But for reception, the cognition of the sleeping person is better because the internal impressions from external movements can be received better when the senses are at rest: "Thus we can understand in this sense that which is said of Balaam in Numbers (24:16): 'Who falling,' that is, sleeping, 'has his eyes opened.'"[19]

In the *ST*, Balaam is used as a scriptural example of a "prophet of demons" who foretells truth. Balaam is appealed to in the *sed contra*, which is noteworthy, as this appeal to authority means that the following facts are not controversial: (a) Balaam was a diviner and sometimes foreknew the future with the help of demons and the art of magic and (b) he foretold the truth. Examples appealed to in the *sed contra* section of an article are generally agreed upon and serve as appeals to authority. In the book of Numbers 24:17, Balaam is said to have prophesied, "A star shall come out of Jacob, and a scepter shall rise out of Israel."[20] Therefore, even the prophets of demons foretell the truth. In the reply in the same article, Thomas clarifies that the prophets of the demons do not always speak from the demons' revelation but sometimes from divine inspiration. He draws on the book of Numbers (22:12) again to show that the Lord spoke to Balaam and instructed him not to curse the Israelites: "God makes use even of the wicked for the profit of the good. Hence He foretells certain truths even by the demons' prophets, both that the truth may be rendered more credible, since even its foes bear witness to it, and also in order that men, by believing such men, may be more easily led on to truth."[21] Thomas adds that even when the demons' prophets are instructed by demons, they can still foretell the truth. This occurs either by virtue of their own nature, the author of which is the Holy Spirit, or by the revelation of good spirits. Even a prophet who is under the influence of a demon can tell a certain truth that arises from the Holy Spirit. It is also noteworthy that Thomas was not alone in considering Balaam a prophet, for one of his objectors, Isidore of Seville, also appeals to Balaam in her explication of the division of prophecy.[22] With Balaam, then, we have a limited-case scenario of the fact that even a demonic prophet can participate—however partially—in the experience of prophecy. God uses whom He wills when trying to communicate with the human race. We might also note, finally, that according to his own criteria, even Thomas might have acknowledged Muhammad to speak prophetically on occasion, for God could use even a false prophet to communicate to His people. As we saw in the opening of chapter 2, Thomas considered Muhammad a false prophet. This is, of course, neither the argument of this book nor an argument that Thomas himself deploys, but it is simply worth noting that according to Thomas's own internal criteria and judgment about Muhammad this possibility could remain open for him.

Solomon

Thomas struggles with ascribing the title of prophet to Solomon throughout his writings. But he ultimately judges that Solomon enjoyed prophetic knowledge about human affairs. In the *Commentary on Hebrews* he prefers the title of "sage" (*sapiens*) to prophet,[23] whereas in the *Commentary on the First Epistle to the Corinthians* and in the *DVer* he recognizes Solomon as a prophet.[24] In the *DVer* he is more explicit than anywhere else about Solomon's prophecy: "Sometimes, therefore, there is no supernatural reception in prophecy, but only supernatural judgment. Thus, the understanding alone is enlightened without any sight of imagination. Perhaps Solomon's inspiration was of this nature, since by a divine impulse he made more certain judgments than the rest of us about human actions and the natures of things, which we perceive naturally."[25] In the *ST* he also claims that Solomon enjoyed prophetic knowledge. The two texts from the *ST* affirm that the King of Israel possessed infused scientific knowledge or wisdom (*scientiam vel sapientiam infusam*)[26] since he was enlightened by an interior light (*ex interiori lumine illustrator*).[27] The prophecy in question here is connected to a special grace that is not a gift of the Holy Spirit but is rather a gratuitous grace given to the intellect. Thomas affirms that an illumined judgment suffices for prophetic revelation. Natural knowledge is formally distinct from knowledge that is obtained naturally through the senses but that is judged by a prophetic light. Solomon represents a limited case with respect to the subject matter known. Generally, prophetic knowledge concerns that which surpasses human reason. But on occasion, God can grant a person the supernatural ability to judge things concerning natural reason. This was the case with Solomon.

CHRIST

In the *Tertia pars* of the *ST*, Thomas entertains the question of whether Jesus enjoyed the gift of prophecy. He begins by defining a prophet as someone who speaks of far-off things, insofar as he knows and announces that which is far from our senses. Thomas reflects on prophecy here with respect to time and space. No one can be called a prophet for knowing and announcing what is distant from others, while he is near to the place. If someone who is living in France, for example, were to know and announce to others living in France what was happening in Syria, it would be prophetic. Thomas's scriptural example is drawn from the Second Book of Kings, where Elisha tells his servant Gehazi that he knows what transpired when he met Naaman at the chariot. The crucial detail here is that Elisha was not there to witness the deception.[28] But if anyone living in Syria were to pronounce to the people who were living in that same place, it would not be prophetic. The same is true with respect to time. It was prophetic of Isaiah to announce that Cyrus, King of the Persians, would rebuild the temple (Is. 44:28). But it was not prophetic of Ezra to write this accomplishment down while the temple was being rebuilt. As a result, if God or the angels or the blessed know and announce what is beyond human knowing, this does not pertain to prophecy since they do not share our state. But Jesus before his passion did share our state "inasmuch as He was not merely a 'comprehensor,' but a 'wayfarer.'"[29] As a result, when He knew and announced what was beyond the knowledge of other "wayfarers," he did so as a prophet. While Balaam's donkey is a limited case in the direction of knowledge of God by animals, we have here a limited case in the other direction. Jesus knew with beatific knowledge,[30] but when he spoke *qua* wayfarer about things beyond the reach of human reason, he spoke prophetically.

The objections to Thomas's arguments in this question of the *ST* are pertinent to our discussion. The first objector understandably concludes that Jesus could not be a prophet since prophetic knowledge implies obscure and imperfect knowledge, but Jesus's knowledge was unveiled and complete. Thomas replies that many in Scripture enjoy the gift of prophecy as enigmatic knowledge. But Moses saw God plainly and is still called a prophet. The stronger part of his response recognizes that while Christ had full and unveiled knowledge in his intellect, his imagination still received knowledge by way of similitudes in the way other wayfarers receive such knowledge. So He could enjoy prophetic knowledge through imaginative forms. The second objector takes data from earlier articles of the same question and applies it to the issue of Christ's prophetic knowledge. Thomas had already established in articles 3 and 4 of the same question that in Christ there could be no faith or hope since faith concerns what is not seen and hope concerns what is not possessed. Prophecy has to do with what is not present, since a prophet is someone who speaks of far-off things. Thomas replies that faith regards things that are unseen by the person who believes, and hope concerns things not possessed by the one who hopes, but prophecy concerns things that are beyond the sense of human beings, "with whom the prophet dwells and converses in this state of life."[31] Consequently, while faith and hope are repugnant to the perfection of Christ's beatitude, prophecy is not. He writes:

> Finally Christ knew by divinely imprinted knowledge:
>
> whatever can be known by force of a man's active intellect, e.g. whatever pertains to human sciences; secondly, by this knowledge Christ knew all things made known to man by Divine revelation, whether they belong to the gift of wisdom or the gift of prophecy, or any other gift of the Holy Ghost; since the soul of Christ knew these things more fully and completely than others.[32]

So Christ, as wayfarer, knew everything that human knowledge could reach and everything imparted by divine revelation, including what is received through prophecy. At one end of the spectrum, Thomas recognized that even a person as evil as Caiaphas could speak prophetically and, at the other end, he recognized that Jesus, who enjoyed beatific knowledge in this life, acted as a prophet when He spoke as a wayfarer about things far from human reason.

MUHAMMAD AMONG THE SCRIPTURAL PROPHETS

For Thomas, whether or not Caiaphas and the Roman soldiers or Balaam or Solomon were properly prophets did not turn on whether they were believers. The issue of belief in relation to Caiaphas and the Roman soldiers does not emerge anywhere in his corpus. Caiaphas enjoyed part of what characterizes prophecy but was not, strictly speaking, a prophet because he spoke without being moved interiorly in his understanding, and he did not truly comprehend what he was saying. Yet he prophesied. In his systematic works, Thomas would apply Augustine's terminology of prophetic instinct to Caiaphas. While he can be said to have enjoyed a "prophetic instinct" since he spoke prophetically, he did not enjoy the full office of prophet. The same is true of the actions of the Roman soldiers. They did not understand the significance of their actions. But both they and Caiaphas participated in the prophetic experience. In the *ST* Thomas clarifies that those enjoying a prophetic instinct can be mistaken about whether their prophecies come from a divine spirit or an evil one, but he admits the same regarding fully fledged prophets. There is more room for error here. But they still participate in the prophetic process for the benefit of others.

What Thomas affirms about prophecy reflects a theme that runs through all four Gospels. Those who recognize Jesus are often the "outsiders," those we would least expect to proclaim Jesus as Lord. And yet the apostles who are the principle evangelizers in the Gospel narratives are often those last to understand the meaning of Jesus's words and actions. In the Gospels of John and Mark in particular, the apostles are a sorry cast of characters who are blind to Jesus's message. God uses them as instruments of His divine power, but in many instances this happens in spite of themselves, not because of their abilities, understanding, or holiness. While it would be going too far astray to enter into a wider scriptural commentary, one cannot help but notice that the theme of "insiders" not understanding who Jesus is while outsiders—even outcasts like lepers and demons, men born blind, and Roman soldiers—do, runs consistently throughout the Gospels. It should not be surprising, then, that what was true during Jesus's lifetime has remained true throughout salvation history. Outsiders might clarify scriptural themes that Christians, while having the source of their salvation staring them in the face, continue to neglect, even as they are categorized as insiders. It has been the task of this chapter and the previous one to suggest that Thomas's account of prophecy accords with this wider scriptural theme.

What do we have at the end of this examination of Thomas's writings on prophecy? We have opened up space on the borders of prophecy where unlikely figures stand. We see that Thomas draws the following concrete conclusions about the prophetic experience:

1. While the reception of corporeal, imaginative, or intellectual images is a central feature of prophecy, the role of judgment is key to prophetic knowledge.

2. Prophecy is a complex category that can include prophetic speech or gestures that do not necessarily exhibit the full sense of prophecy.
3. Prophets have emerged in history since the death of Jesus; "at all times" there have been prophets, especially those aiding the direction of human acts.
4. Unbelievers can speak and act prophetically.
5. True prophets cannot always distinguish between what is from a divine spirit and what is from an evil one.
6. One and the same prophet can receive prophetic knowledge in one way at a certain point and in another way at another moment.
7. Prophets can misunderstand or misuse true prophetic knowledge.
8. Sometimes a person can enjoy a certain prophetic instinct but not always fully distinguish between human and divine elements of the prophetic knowledge.
9. Even evil spirits can speak prophetically.
10. Sometimes a prophetic light is necessary even regarding things that can be known by natural reason.

Theologians regularly cite Thomas in affirming that the goal of prophecy is to direct human activity,[33] but Hvidt argues that prophecy is also directed toward understanding Christian revelation more adequately: "Christian prophecy is not revelation on par with the Bible, but this does not mean that it cannot serve as verification of and support for revelation. Postcanonical Christian prophecy can indeed serve to elucidate points of Scripture that are not clear or that Scripture contains in an implicit way only, and as such it can and has indeed played a very important role in the correction and actualization of our understanding of revelation."[34] This book suggests that we extend Hvidt's conclusions about postcanonical Christian prophecy to include possible non-Christian prophetic experiences. It might be that outsiders to the Christian tradition are offered roles of elucidating Christian revelation in a way that can come only from outsiders. This pattern already emerged in Scripture. It should come as no surprise that it has continued past the closing of the canon.

In reflecting upon *DV*, the Pontifical Council for Interreligious Dialogue agrees. Christians still grow into the realities of Scripture in a continual and dynamic process. Interreligious dialogue becomes integral to this work, as "God, in an age-long dialogue, has offered and continues to offer salvation to humankind. In faithfulness to this divine initiative, the Church too must enter into a dialogue of salvation with all men and women."[35]

We have seen how the documents of the Second Vatican Council put forth this dynamic model of revelation that will continue to unfold until the end of time. Those documents also affirmed that Christians and Muslims adore the one God together, and even share substantive theological claims. We can now add that a medieval account of prophecy offers an expansive account of the prophetic experience, where even some who do not believe in Jesus act and speak prophetically. The criterion for prophetic knowledge lies not in the assent of faith, but rather in the process by which the knowledge is received and imparted to others. God chooses the most unlikely figures, even within the pages of Scripture, to speak and act prophetically. At this point, it is a theoretical possibility that Muhammad enjoyed a prophetic instinct *at least* like that of Caiaphas or the Roman soldiers. God could have chosen Muhammad in some moments to strengthen his intellect in order to understand things that accord with natural reason (as in the case of Solomon); in other moments, God could have chosen Muhammad to speak prophetically without fully understanding what he was saying (as in the case of Caiaphas). In yet further moments, Muhammad could have mixed some of his own instincts with a divine prophecy he had received. And it is of course altogether possible under Thomas's account that God chose Muhammad to speak prophetically.

Accepting the possibility of Muhammad's prophethood in these Christian terms does not lead to a wholesale adoption of the Qur'an as revelation alongside the Christian Scripture. While certainly not all the claims in the Qur'an accord with the Christian Scriptures, the overlapping web of belief is wide enough to suggest the possibility that the God of Abraham, Isaac, and Jacob revealed divine messages to Muhammad through the angel Gabriel in seventh-century Arabia. In fact, Thomas's analysis, wed to Vatican II claims about Muslims, places Muhammad closer to Christian prophecy than even Caiaphas, the Roman soldiers, or Balaam, and perhaps, as he himself claimed to his original listeners, closer to the Hebrew prophets who spoke to a particular place and people. The substance of shared beliefs and the claim that Muhammad received these messages from the angel Gabriel lead us at least to consider the possibility that Muhammad was a postcanonical prophet who addressed pagans, Christians, and Jews of seventh-century Arabia. This theoretical openness means that Christians should take the Qur'an theologically seriously.

The next chapter outlines the writings of four Christian thinkers who have deeply examined Muslim thought and practice, have entertained the governing question of this book, and have answered in the affirmative. We then examine the writings of two thinkers who reached negative conclusions on this same question. We critically examine each of these options before drawing some conclusions of our own in the final chapter, conclusions that speak to the particular question set forth in this book and open up into wider areas of inquiry in the theology of religious pluralism that require further research.

CHAPTER FIVE

Is Muhammad a Prophet
for Christians?

Joining the Conversation

Once the theoretical possibility of Muhammad's prophecy has been established through an examination of unresolved questions from Vatican II and retrieval of a medieval account of prophecy, I will turn to concrete discernment about whether Christians could in fact consider Muhammad a prophet. I will examine the writings of some notable Christian theologians from the past fifty years who have considered this question. I review their starting points, approaches, and conclusions. Each of the first four thinkers offers a particular model through which to consider Muhammad's prophecy, although there are some significant areas of overlap among their proposals. The final two thinkers who have considered this question conclude that Christians should not ascribe the title "prophet" to Muhammad. We critically examine the reasons behind their reluctance and conclude by offering possible inroads into further development of this question.[1] The next chapter will recapture the argument of this book and show how it is a fruitful alternative to the approaches of the thinkers examined below.

MUHAMMAD AS MORAL PROPHET

William Montgomery Watt—a Scottish historian, orientalist, and Anglican priest—was probably the most distinguished Islam specialist from the last century. His classic *Muhammad at Mecca* (1953) and *Muhammad at Medina* (1956) have become indispensable reading for Western students of Islam, and he is regarded as the most prolific Western scholar of *sīra* scholarship. While the bulk of his scholarship is historical, toward the latter half of his career he turned to theological questions that had been cropping up throughout his work. These included an explicit consideration of the question about Muhammad's prophethood. A reader can find throughout his corpus consistent themes and convictions around this question. In asking whether Christians can consider Muhammad a prophet, Watt reflected first on Muhammad's historical personality, second on the community he founded, and third on the book that documented his revelations. We will take each in turn.

Watt was convinced from early on in his career that Muhammad was sincere in his belief about his reception of divine revelations and confident in his ability to distinguish between his own thoughts and the divine messages he received through the angel Gabriel. Muhammad would not have been able to carry out his mission in the face of such adversity and hostility unless he truly believed that God had entrusted him with this task. Sincerity of belief, however, does not imply correct belief. One could be completely sincere in one's conviction that it is in fact the angel Gabriel who speaks and yet mistaken in the actual fact of the matter: "What seems to a man to come from 'outside himself' may actually come from his unconscious."[2] Watt then—less convincingly—concluded that God could not have allowed a great religion like Islam to develop on the "basis of lies and deceit."[3]

Sincerity of belief was only the first step in an examination of the character of Muhammad. Watt examined the issue of his moral exemplarity with somewhat mixed results. On the one hand, he admitted that Muhammad's contemporaries certainly considered him *the* moral exemplar. A whole tradition of *sīra* literature emerged during the ensuing centuries around this conviction. In addition, Watt argued that Muhammad's standards of behavior were higher than those of the culture of his day. He was a social reformer—even in the area of morality—inventing a system of social security and a new family structure. He thereby improved on the social habits of pre-Islamic Arabs. He took the best in Arabian nomadic culture and adapted it to the lives of settled communities.[4] On the other hand, Muslims claim that Muhammad was a *universal* moral exemplar whose teachings are applicable to all times and ages. Here Watt hesitated to agree with his Muslim interlocutors. He suggested that Muslims have yet to convince Westerners that Muhammad continues to contribute to the moral development of humanity, but he recognized that his Muslim followers today can contribute to the wider world "for they have retained emphases—on the reality of God, for example—which have been neglected or forgotten in important sections of other monotheistic religions."[5]

To sincerity of beliefs and moral exemplarity Watt added Muhammad's quality of being a "seer." Without exactly commending the orthodox Muslim view that Muhammad's revelations came from God, Watt suggested that his revelations enabled him to resolve the social tensions of his day. These revelations correctly diagnosed social ills and were dressed in such a way that they moved his followers to revere his leadership capacities. While the Qur'an might not have been suited to twentieth-century Europeans, Watt admits, it was admirably matched to the cultural conditions of seventh-century Arabia.

Muhammad was also a gifted administrator and statesman. He was able to turn the conceptual framework of his revelations into concrete political strategies and social reforms that lasted well beyond his death. One need only glance at a map of the growth of Islam within its first hundred years to recognize Muhammad's political and military skill. Watt remarks, "His wisdom in these matters is shown by the rapid expansion of his small state to a world-empire after his death, and by the adaptation of his social institutions to many different environments and their continuance for thirteen centuries."[6] Even if Muhammad had not clearly selected a successor by the time of his death, he had put enough social structures in place that his followers were able to turn Islam from a small religious community into a powerful religious empire.[7]

But the historical evidence only goes so far. Watt recognizes that this question of Muhammad's prophethood demands a theological judgment. He ascribes to Muhammad a "creative imagination," much like that of artists, poets, and writers: "All these put into sensuous form (pictures, poems, dramas, novels) what many are feeling but are unable to express fully. Great works of the creative imagination have thus a certain universality, in that they give expression to the feelings and attitudes of a whole generation. They are, of course, not imaginary, for they deal with real things; but they employ images, visual or conjured up by words, to express what is beyond the range of man's intellectual conceptions."[8] A true prophet successfully deploys her creative imagination for the benefit of her surrounding community. What distinguishes someone with real creative imagination from an imposter? True creative thinkers offer ideas that have actual purchase for those to whom they are addressed. Concerning prophets in particular, Watt leaves open the possibility that these ideas could emerge from the unconscious, although religious believers would ascribe these ideas to God. For his part, Watt suggests that perhaps "these ideas of the creative imagination come from that life in a man which is greater than himself and is largely below the threshold of consciousness."[9] Was Muhammad, then, a true prophet? Watt concludes: "He was a man in whom creative imagination worked at deep levels and produced ideas relevant to the central questions of human existence so that his religion has had a widespread appeal, not only in his own age but in succeeding centuries. Not all the ideas he proclaimed are true and sound, but by God's grace he has been enabled to provide millions of men with a better religion than they had before they testified that there is no god but God and that Muhammad is the messenger of God."[10] So, already by the early 1960s, Watt was able to ascribe the title of "prophet" to Muhammad insofar as one accepts the above portrayal of what a prophet means to a religious tradition.

It is an open question, of course, whether religious believers—Muslims or otherwise—would accept this description of a prophet. If "creative imagination" and the ability to provide Muslims with a better religion than they would otherwise have had is enough to raise someone to the status of prophethood, one wonders how many other poets of the world would fit this expansive description. Muslims are not the only ones who would reject this conception of prophecy. *Any* religious believer would recognize that Watt's understanding of prophecy has hollowed out all references to the transcendental dimension of human existence. *All* religious believers would object to having their beliefs severed from the supernatural reaches of their fundamental claims.

We have seen how an examination of Muhammad's character led Watt to conclude that he can justifiably be called a prophet. But his analysis does not end there. As a second arena for consideration, Watt turns to the effects that Muhammad had on succeeding generations and deploys the biblical discernment criteria of "you shall know them by their fruits" (Mt. 7:16). Since religious language is largely iconic, there can be "no intellectual criterion which enables one to compare religions in respect of truth and falsehood, or even relative truth and false-hood."[11] In its place, Watt offers the practical criterion of "fruits," writing: "If the quality of life is in general good, then it can be said that the system of belief is more or less true."[12] Instead of conceptual truth, then, the criterion becomes whether the lives lived are "satisfactory" or "adequate." By the time Muhammad died, he left thousands of follow-ers, who have grown to over a billion in the modern world, comprising one-fifth of the world's population. Muslims' quality of life has been "on the whole satisfactory for the members."[13] How can this be mea-sured? Generally, Muslims can be said to live decent and relatively happy lives under difficult circumstances.[14] Watt suggests, "These points lead to the conclusion that the view of reality presented in the Qur'ān is true and from God, and therefore Muhammad is a genuine prophet."[15] These lives are meaningful and harmonious, despite the effects of pain and suffering. Watt admits that this criterion could never be applied with "mathematical rigour," but he assumes that people from different cultures could largely agree as to what constitutes "good fruit."[16] In a later work, Watt suggests that Islam has led millions of Muslims to live better lives than they would otherwise have lived,[17] even if this, too, is impervious to measurement.

But why did Christianity not do the work of improving the lives of seventh-century Arabs? The Qur'an presumes knowledge of bibli-cal history, and historical evidence points to the fact that Muhammad knew about Christianity and met Jews in Mecca, Medina, and beyond. Watt argues that the Christianity of Muhammad's day had a number of important weaknesses. The Arabs of Mecca had recently come to enjoy an economic boom and found their old way of life breaking down. They required something new, but "none of the existing forms of Christianity was able to meet their needs," and there was "a religious vacuum in Mecca" that Christians had not been able to fill.[18] Watt further argues that the rapid expansion of Islam into North Africa, the Fertile Crescent, and Iran suggests that these regions also suffered from something like a religious vacuum. He concludes: "There are thus grounds for holding that God was behind the appearance of Islam in order to bring something better to the people involved. In other words, Islam came into being, not through human planning but by divine initiative. If a divine initiative is admitted, it has then to be asked how God worked through Muhammad."[19] Add to this that a rift had developed between the Greek or Hellenized Christians of the Roman or Byzantine Empire and the Semitic and less Hellenized Christians from the East. During this rift, the religion of Muhammad emerged as an attractive religious alternative.[20]

While Watt's primary areas of consideration in answering our question concern Muhammad's life trajectory and the quality of living of subsequent Muslim generations, he does occasionally turn to the text of the Qur'an to see if it can help provide an answer. A problem immediately emerges insofar as Muslims and Christians have conflicting perceptions of the role of the Qur'an in world history. Watt insists that the Qur'an presents itself as an *Arabic* text, and in so doing reveals its geographic and historical contours. The revelations, emerging as they do in Arabic, need to be translated to people of different times and places. The words themselves belie their historical situatedness.[21] But Muslims deny that the revelations are meant for a particular time and place; instead, they believe that they are divine words meant for a universal audience. Christians understand a prophet to be directed to a particular time and place in history. Muslims, rather, believe that prophets receive the actual words of God without any human element mixed into the revelations.[22] Against the Muslim reading, Watt insists that the text refers to seventh-century events such as the battles at Badr and Uhud, revealing their historical context. Watt's account would also leave room for mistaken statements about biblical matters in the Qur'an, for if each word in the Qur'an is divine, there is no room for error, even about historical matters. On the whole, however, Watt encourages Christians to find positive value in the Qur'an and to recognize there many teachings that cohere with central Christian beliefs.[23]

After reviewing the quality of Muhammad's character, the religious movement he inaugurated, and the text that documented his received revelations, Watt is able to conclude that Muhammad "is a religious leader through whom God has worked, and that is tantamount to holding that he is in some sense a prophet."[24] Watt does not agree with the Muslim belief in the infallibility of Muhammad's revelations, for he cannot accept any part of the Qur'an that conflicts with central Christian beliefs. He is most comfortable reading the Qur'an as a body of ideas and examining their significance in their social and historical context.[25]

These considerations about Muhammad lead Watt to conclude that religions are complementary to one another, each bearing witness to some aspect of divine truth that is not fully expressed in the others. Members of an individual religious tradition can believe that their rendition of divine truth is more important than any other, but ultimately, religions have emerged throughout world history in response to particular cultural and religious needs.[26] According to the accepted typology in the theology of religious pluralism, Watt subcribes to the model of "pluralism" in religious belief. Pluralists maintain that religious traditions are independently valid paths to salvation and that Christ is irrelevant to those traditions, although He serves Christians as their means to salvation. The challenge of subscribing to this typology is that it minimizes religious difference and suspends any sort of truth judgment about religious belief. One wonders the worth of the invitation extended to Muhammad to become a prophet in Montgomery Watt's sense of the word, since his understanding of prophecy would not satisfy traditional Christians, Muslims, or Jews. In an important sense, Christian religious pluralists who ascribe the title of "prophet" to Muhammad do so only by evacuating it of any real transcendental meaning. Without the possibility of transcendence, prophets cannot truly prophecy.

MUHAMMAD AS PROPHET AGAINST IDOLATRY

Hans Küng is a Swiss Roman Catholic priest and theologian who has done important work in ecumenical theology over the course of his career. As a result of his rejection of the doctrine of papal infallibility, he had to leave the Catholic faculty at the University of Tübingen, but he remained a member of the ecumenical faculty until his retirement in 1996. His later work is what interests us here, as it moved into areas of interreligious dialogue and the creation of a global ethic. He became interested in Islam in particular in the early 1980s, when he considered the question of Muhammad's prophethood. Our discussion of his oeuvre, then, will concentrate mostly on his work during that time.

In 1986, when reflecting upon the Second Vatican Council's pronouncements on Islam, Küng openly criticized the bishops for omitting any mention of Muhammad in their positive references to Muslims: "The same church must, in my opinion, also respect the one whose name is absent from the same declaration out of embarrassment, although he and he alone led Muslims to pray to this one God, so that once again through him, Muhammad, the Prophet, this God has spoken to mankind."[27] He also encouraged Christians to acknowledge Muhammad as an "authentic (post-Christian) prophet and his 'warning' about a declension from belief in one God in Christianity."[28] Muhammad here serves to remind Christians to be vigilant against idolatry.

For Küng, Muhammad represents a radical rupture with the past. The revelations compiled in the Qur'an are an "epochal turning point" in the history of Arabia: "Muhammad is discontinuity in person, an ultimately irreducible figure, who cannot be simply derived from what preceded him, but stands radically apart from it as he, with the Qur'an, establishes permanent new standards. In that respect, Muhammad and the Qur'an represent a decisive break, a departure from the past, a shift toward a new future."[29] In Muhammad's role as prophet, he entered into the stream of the history of religions and changed its course. Muhammad came to function as a "religious archetype" for a large segment of the world's population.[30] In fact, when people speak "of '*the* prophet,' *tout court*, of a man who claimed to be *that* but absolutely nothing more, then there can be no doubt that this is Muhammad."[31]

Küng finds certain striking parallels between Muhammad and the prophets of Israel. They all based their work not on any official office designated by their surrounding communities but rather on their special relationships with God. They were all strong-willed, understanding themselves as "wholly penetrated by [their] divine vocation."[32]

They spoke in the midst of religious and social crises and stood up against the wealthy ruling class. They understood themselves as speaking for God, and not in their own words. They adored the one, creator, merciful God and admonished idolatrous worship. They insisted upon unconditional obedience to God and generosity toward their fellow human beings. They all linked their religious faith with the work of social justice.[33] Küng concludes that the God of the Qur'an and the Hebrew scriptures speaks through both with one voice. As a result, recognizing prophets like Amos and Hosea or Isaiah and Jeremiah but not Muhammad above all emerges from a certain "dogmatic prejudice."[34]

Küng urges Christians to acknowledge three important aspects of Islam. First, seventh-century Arabs were justified in taking Muhammad seriously. Second, they were introduced to monotheism and purged of "this-worldly" polytheism of pre-Islamic tribal religions in the region. Finally, they received from Muhammad the inspiration, courage, and strength needed to inaugurate a new religion. They came to understand and know God more deeply and thereby revitalized their religious traditions.[35]

Küng also remarks that the Hebrew prophets varied greatly one from the other, and some of them led unsaintly lives. Also, the New Testament testifies to the fact that authentic prophets preached *after* the death of Jesus, "men and women who attested to him and his message, who interpreted and translated it for a new age and a new situation."[36]

Küng concludes that Christians should heed Muhammad's call to worship the one God, to reject idolatry, and to bring faith into every sphere of life, including politics. Muhammad came as a "prophetic corrective" or a "prophetic warner."[37] Küng goes so far as to say that a decision for Jesus is a decision for his follower Muhammad insofar as he preached about the same God as Jesus did.[38]

Küng produced three important books on the Abrahamic religions in the 1990's, on Judaism (1991), Christianity (1999), and Islam (2004). His ambitious *Islam: Past, Present and Future* takes up the question of Muhammad's prophecy and reaffirms his positive evaluation of the prophet. While the book as a whole is historically driven, organized along a series of paradigm shifts throughout the history of Islam, Küng briefly takes up the theological question of prophecy. He argues that Muhammad was convinced of his own prophetic authenticity and that he could have enjoyed a comfortable merchant life instead of the trials and travels that he undertook as the emerging leader of this new religious movement.[39] Küng, in fact, suggests that if we dispute the authenticity of Muhammad's revelation, should we not also dispute the authenticity of the revelations of Israel's prophets, even of Jesus of Nazareth?[40] He then lists several parallels between the prophets of Israel and Muhammad and concludes that the three revelatory religions of Semitic origin—especially those based on the Hebrew Bible and the Qur'an—all have the same basis. He reaffirms his earlier conviction that it is simply "dogmatic prejudice" for Christians to recognize as prophets Amos and Hosea or Isaiah and Jeremiah but not Muhammad.[41] While details of the relationship between Jesus and Muhammad still need to be clarified, he admits, recognizing Muhammad as a prophet would "have major positive consequences for an understanding between Christians and Muslims."[42]

Küng joins Watt in his assessment of Muhammad's prophecy and shares Watt's underlying theological presuppositions of religious pluralism. However, he accentuates Muhammad's role in purifying Christian belief and practice by preaching against idolatry, which he holds to be a perennial temptation for Christians. Christians who subcribe to religious pluralism might not need more convincing. The argument of this book, however, does not begin from this presupposition. Instead, it takes as its starting point the documents of the Catholic Church, including *Dominus Iesus* (2000), which states unequivocally the universal salvific significance of Jesus Christ. In doing this, it takes seriously Muslim claims to the universal scope of their own religious beliefs in a way that the proposals by Watt and Küng fail to do.

MUHAMMAD AS PROPHET OF THE QUR'AN

Anglican bishop and scholar Kenneth Cragg is a key figure in twentieth-century Christian approaches to Islam. His numerous books exhibit over fifty years of theological engagement with the Qur'an and the history of Islam. He has written in the areas of Islamic studies,

Christian-Muslim relations, and interfaith dialogue. He served the Church of England in Oxford, Jerusalem, and Cairo and worked in academic contexts in Beirut, Hartford, Connecticut, Ibadan, and Sussex. The fruits of this labor can be seen in his most famous work, *The Call of the Minaret* (1956), but also in the comparative readings of Muslim and Christian Scriptures found in *A Certain Sympathy of Scriptures: Biblical and Qur'anic* (2004) and in the theological engagement of the compatibility between Islam and the West in *The Qur'an and the West* (2005), among many other works. The most important work for the argument of this book is his *Muhammad and the Christian: A Question of Response* (1999), where he explicitly undertakes the question of whether Christians should consider Muhammad a prophet. He concludes, somewhat controversially, that Muhammad can be viewed by Christians as the "Prophet of the Qur'an."

Before turning to the earlier *Muhammad and the Christian* (1984), however, we should mention that already in the 1950s Cragg had begun to address this question in *The Call of the Minaret*. Cragg is unapologetic there and elsewhere in judging the issue of prophethood from the confessional perspective of Christianity.[43] In fact, he finds in the Qur'an itself (5:47)[44] warrant for judging the truth of the Qur'an through the light of the Gospel.[45] He admittedly takes *injīl* (gospel) here in a looser sense than is generally read by Muslims, for he does not think it should refer *only* to the Gospel revealed to Jesus spoken of in the Qur'an but rather to the Gospel as it has come down to Christians. He concludes: "The Muhammadan decision here is formative of all else in Islam. It was a decision for community, for resistance, for external victory, for pacification and rule. The decision of the Cross—no less conscious, no less formative, no less inclusive—was the contrary decision."[46] Throughout his later works Cragg remains uneasy about the Islamic decision to take up the sword and embrace political power.[47] He also maintains a distinction between the two meanings of *Islam* or "submission," the first being the interior, personal and laudatory, and religious submission and the second the visible submission to a political power, which he finds highly problematic.[48]

Cragg's method of discerning the possible prophethood of Muhammad is a Qur'anic one. He adopts a different approach to Watts's consideration of Muhammad's life and legacy. He relegates issues of

Muhammad's personality, history, and career to a secondary plane and chooses to focus instead on the content of the Qur'an itself, a text that he had long studied. This move frees him from the tangles of early Muslim scholarship and political history and largely circumscribes his task, although it also opens him up to Muslim critique of his Western methods of interpretation. He is able to conclude that Muhammad was a "prophet of the Qur'an." What does he mean by this? While Jews and Christians were not able to make significant inroads in seventh-century Arabia, Muhammad succeeded in bringing a message resonant with Jews and Christians to the Bedouin tribes of this desert: "In estimating Muhammad's role in seventh-century (A.D.) Mecca/Medina one has to consider not only the years but the cities, not simply the date but the locale. . . . Prophetic meanings that might seem retrogressive by simple time criteria may be progressive by those of place and culture."[49] In other words, Muhammad can be understood as a prophet to a particular people and culture. He can therefore be compared to prophets of the Old Testament, for while seventh-century Arabs lived well after the birth of Jesus, the message of Christianity had not been able to reach them yet in a compelling way. Where Judaism and Christianity failed, Islam succeeded.

Cragg does not mean to agree here with traditional Muslim interpretations of the way that Muhammad heard and recorded these revelations. Instead, he interprets Qur'anic experience of prophethood as a "deep human experience under a directing sense of divine transcendence."[50] The Qur'anic text expresses its shapes and contours through the historical context of seventh-century Arabia. And yet "there can be no doubt (unless of a tendentious kind) that the Qur'an constitutes a massive document of religious meaning whose deepest sources lie beyond personal human factors."[51]

While Cragg has been criticized for limiting Muhammad's prophetic role to Muslims,[52] he does not argue that Muhammad's prophetic revelations brought the biblical heritage only to Arabia. Instead, they should also be heeded today by modern people generally and by Jews and Christians in particular. The Qur'an's call to reject all idolatrous worship in favor of the unity of God is one that needs heeding today, since idolatry is the "besetting evil" of the modern world.[53] These revelations also call moderns to reject the bifurcation between sacred and secular, as they call believers to bring right reverence to quotidian life. Cragg insists:

> But the same "signs" which thus admit of the scientific empire of man also call him to religious reverence. The same signs. The point is important. There is no proper division between the work and worship, between authority and submission. Where man takes his dominion, he must present his praise. The *āyāt* [signs] which educate the researcher, require the laboratory, and give rise to the economy, must also point towards the sanctuary. . . . Quranic theism teaches a unity of divine will and mercy behind all plural things and so directs all instinct of dependence, wonder, praise and reliance towards that one centre of a right adoration.[54]

While Cragg admits that Muhammad's original message transformed a particular time and place, he is unmistakable in urging his contemporaries to heed the admonishments and encouragements of God in the Qur'an.

Cragg concludes his study, however, with a few cautionary notes. While his appreciation for Muhammad as a prophet is meant to encourage Christians to encounter the Qur'an more deeply, he recognizes that as an outsider he cannot truly penetrate the interiority of the Muslim faith, for, in the end, the "*imitatio Muhammadi*" and the "*imitatio Christi*" are two fundamentally different alternatives.[55] But he also leaves the reader with three tantalizing questions: "Can there be a unity of spirit beyond, or even despite, a lack of unity in doctrine? Can a community of fellowship reach outside a community of faith? Is faith itself shared even when it is at issue?"[56]

In his later work, Cragg does not waver from his embrace of Muhammad as a prophet, but he cannot help but wonder why the Qur'an omits mentioning crucial Old Testament prophets like Hosea and Isaiah or Jeremiah, Ezekiel, and Malachi. He conjectures that the more successful patriarchs like Noah, Abraham, Moses, and David fit more neatly into the vigorous political action sanctioned by the Qur'an, while the irony of a Hosea and Jeremiah "would have had no purchase on minds in Mecca."⁵⁷ The psychology of these latter prophets might not have fit Qur'anic patterns. Cragg is suggestive here, not determinative. But he does conclude that this omission makes a comparison with Muhammad both more challenging and more necessary. We see in Cragg a Christian theologian who takes the doctrinal differences between Muslims and Christians seriously and invites Christians to join him in studying the Qur'an through Christian lenses. The important theological question that Cragg asks us to consider is taken up in this book: "Is faith itself shared even when it is at issue?"⁵⁸ In some ways, then, Cragg's work on the question of the prophethood of Muhammad can be seen as preliminary to the work of this book. Further, the invitation to take the Qur'an theologically seriously, with which this book concludes, is one that Cragg has already accepted and in which he has shown himself a pioneer.

MUHAMMAD AS LIBERATOR

David Kerr was an internationally renowned scholar in the field of interreligious dialogue and Islamic-Christian relations. He directed two important Christian-Muslim study centers, the Center for the Study of Islam and Christian Muslim Relations (in Birmingham, England) and the D. B. Macdonald Center (in Hartford, Connecticut). In 1996 he was appointed professor of Christianity in the Non-Western World at the University of Edinburgh, Scotland. He moved to Lund University in 2005, where he held the chair in missiology until his untimely death in 2008. Kerr's research focused on the relationship between Christianity and Islam. He published important work on the intersection between liberation theology in Christianity and political theology in Islam. He offers the model of "Muhammad as Liberator" as he considers whether, from the perspective of Christianity, Muhammad can be understood to be a prophet.

Kerr wrote three important essays addressing the prophethood of Muhammad. In the first, "The Prophet Muhammad in Christian Theological Perspective" (1991), he argues that Christians should appreciate Muhammad's ministry ethically and reexamine what prophethood means from the perspective of religious pluralism. In a second essay, "He Walked in the Path of the Prophets: Toward a Christian Theological Recognition of the Prophethood of Muhammad" (1995), Kerr examines the works of some twentieth-century Christian theologians who developed positive appraisals of Muhammad's prophethood. In the final and most constructive piece, "Muhammad: Prophet of Liberation—A Christian Perspective from Political Theology" (2011), he argues that political theology offers Christians new ways to think about Muhammad. We will examine each piece in turn.

In his 1991 piece, Kerr reviews the history of Christian appraisals of Muhammad's prophecy from John of Damascus (d. 749), who analyzed Islam as a heresy that derived from Christianity but ultimately deviated from orthodoxy, through medieval caricatures of the prophet to nineteenth-century reassessments, most notably Thomas Carlyle's series of lectures in 1840, which portrayed Muhammad as a prophet who aimed at truth and justice. He reviews twentieth-century attempts by Christian theologians to rescue Muhammad from medieval polemics, including those of the historian William Montgomery Watt and the theologian Kenneth Cragg (examined above). Kerr concludes that twentieth-century Protestant reappraisals of Muhammad "consciously attempted to step outside the polemical tradition in accepting Muhammad as a man of religious genius who affected the course of human history under the sovereign rule of God; in this sense he was a man of prophetic inspiration, but in the light of Christ and the gospel his prophethood is attenuated by the ambiguities of temporal power in Medina."[59] In Kerr's estimation, twentieth-century Catholic thought takes us no further. The disappointing claims of Vatican II, which even omit Muhammad and Islam in favor of general references to Muslim beliefs, have not been developed by Catholic thinkers of the past several decades. He asks whether it is possible for Christian theologians to go further in their recognition of the prophethood of Muhammad without themselves becoming Muslim. In asking this question, however, he wonders whether Christians can "go deeper into biblical understanding of divine revelation throughout human history, stripping away the sociopolitical overtones of medieval European thought, so as to avail themselves of new perceptions of the place of other religions,

Islam included, in providential history."[60] Kerr concludes that since God left no people without witnesses to his universal revelation, Christians should explore the extrabiblical testimonies, "searching them for complementary signs of the mystery of divine providence and critically adopting them into its own doxology."[61] Muhammad, he proposes, was such a sign of divine providence to the human race in salvation history.

Kerr's 1995 piece reviews the work of Christian scholars from the mid–twentieth century who have engaged Muhammad as a "post-Christian" prophet, hoping to pursue new possibilities of an "inclusive" approach to Muhammad. Kerr summarizes an impressive amount of scholarly literature by reviewing the work of Louis Massignon, Charles Ledit, Michel Hayek, George Khodr, Kenneth Cragg, Hans Küng, and William Montgomery Watt. Among the inclusivists he finds at least three variants. The first is "an eschatological focus which treats Muhammad as the extra-Christian witness to Christ's Second Coming as Messiah—a theory for which Massignon finds corroboration in the Qur'an, Ledit in an interpretation of Thomist categories of prophethood, and Hayek in an analogical reflection on Ishmael."[62] The second is "a messianic focus which, as Cragg exemplifies, addresses the human condition in the order of mundane history and assesses Muhammad's prophethood to have been genuine but rather less than the 'more than a prophet' New Testament witness of Jesus." And finally, a third is a "pneumatological focus which relates Muhammad to the 'economy of the Holy Spirit' in Khodr's interpretation of the 'catholicity' of Arab culture."[63] Küng and Watt offer a pluralist alternative that is theistic rather than Christic in orientation, offering many authentic paths to God. They invoke ethically pragmatic criteria and apply these both to the Qur'an and to the history of Islam. They operate within a "history of dialectic" paradigm rather than that of a "history of salvation."[64]

Kerr concludes that all seven figures fail to address Islamic understanding of prophecy and prophethood, but, more significantly, they treat the Muhammad of history while neglecting the "Muhammad of Islamic doctrine, piety, prayer and politics."[65] Kerr leaves the reader with the suggestion that contemporary liberation theology might offer new Christian perspectives on Muhammad.

This suggestion he turns into a concrete proposal in the final essay on this topic, "Muhammad: Prophet of Liberation" (2011). Kerr argues that Christians have theological reasons to acknowledge Muhammad as a prophet because Muhammad participated in the "liberative process of transforming human history into the kingdom of God"; he was, therefore, "an ally not a foe of Jesus."[66] Kerr justifies his choice of political theology as a lens through which to examine this issue by first revealing its Christian roots in a 1960s theology that fought social injustice through a renewed biblical hermeneutic. These first arose in the liberation theology of Latin America, Black theology of the United States and South Africa, and feminist theology in northern contexts. While the term "political theology" arose in Christian contexts, other religions do not lack such theology. Islam, in fact, represents a political theology "par excellence." In fact, "its roots go back to the time of the Prophet Muhammad whose preaching of ethical monotheism in Mecca (610–622) culminated in the creation of a new socio-political community in Medina (622–632)."[67] The moral character of government and political life is absolutely central to Islamic religious thought.

Kerr reviews the writings of three contemporary figures who have considered the prophethood of Muhammad through the lens of political theology. William Montgomery Watt came to appreciate Muhammad's originality in his ability to Arabicize the Judeo-Christian tradition in seventh-century Arabia. While Muslims and Christians worship the same God, their ways of understanding this God are shaped by their particular cultural contexts. Watt evaluates religions "in the domain of ethics, the exposition of truth in the practice of living," and here he finds that Islam has given moral purpose to generations of Muslims.[68] On this account, Muhammad can be recognized as a prophet. His maxim "By their fruits you will know them" leads him in his discernment of Muslim belief and practice.

Hans Küng offers a "prophetic corrective" to Christians by reminding them of the "original Semitic character of their faith, and of the Jewish-Christian witness to Jesus."[69] Muhammad, then, becomes "a witness to Jesus," and Islam is "interwoven with Christianity."[70]

For George Khodr, Muhammad's prophetic genius is found in his "vision of radical inclusivity of Arabism." Abraham is the point of reference here, which universalizes the "Islamic revelation" and, in turn, affirms "Biblical catholicity" in the cultural context of Arabia.[71] Khodr maintains that Muslims arrive at true knowledge and experience of

God through the Holy Spirit. Muhammad is united to Christ through a "hidden bond" that will come to light at Christ's second coming.[72]

All three scholars whose work Kerr reviews take political theology seriously in their analysis of Muhammad's prophethood. Watt prioritizes Muhammad's "contextual ethics that transformed unruly Arab tribes into a new ethical community."[73] This gave birth to a religious movement that has long contributed to the common good. Küng interprets the good at work in Islam through the "salvific efficacy of grace, seeing Muhammad's leadership as evidence of the Biblical assurance that 'God has nowhere left Himself [sic] without witnesses' (Acts 15:17)."[74] Khodr is the most specifically sociopolitical, focusing on Muhammad's establishment of an Arabism that includes the three heirs of the Abrahamic religion.

These three theologians affirm Muhammad as a genuine prophet through the socioethical significance of Muhammad's teaching. While none of them explicitly writes from the perspective of political theology, they do appreciate Muhammad's political context. In the most constructive part of the essay, Kerr draws on the work of Gustavo Gutierrez to show that Christians have solid theological reasons to acknowledge Muhammad as a prophet. Muhammad sought to build a radically new society, one that would abide by the ethical standards by which God judges humanity. In this new community, faith in the one God would take priority over tribe and religion. Drawing on the work of Farid Esack, Kerr concludes: "Here lies Muhammad's genius as a peacemaker and political leader: the peace of Medina united the migrants (muhâjirûn) who had been oppressed in Mecca with the new converts in Medina (ansâr) in a system of fraternity (mu'âkhâ) that established economic justice in the community."[75] Christian theologians can find here deep resonances with the modern movement of liberation theology. Drawing on the work of Gustavo Gutierrez, Kerr suggests that liberation theology's prophets "are liberators, God's agents who, in particular historical circumstances, concretise the dynamic of salvation-as-liberation that runs through human history as the corollary of creation itself."[76] This understanding of prophecy finds real kinship with its Muslim counterpart. In both, the reign of God is brought about through an interplay between "divine initiative and human struggle," where the poor or *mustad'afûn* serve as the meeting point between the two.[77] Kerr concludes that Muhammad was a "master of contextual theology" both by enculturating the Abrahamic faith in the context of seventh-century Arabia and by transforming that sociopolitical context in theologically liberative terms.[78]

Kerr then entertains three questions regarding his proposal. The first concerns the recurring issue of Christology. How can Christians consider Muhammad a prophet when he denies the central claim of the Christian faith, namely, that God became flesh, dwelt among us, and thereby restored us in right relationship to each other and to God? Kerr maintains that a creedal approach to this question perpetuates disparity and conflict. Instead, the perspective of the praxis of political theology bypasses these doctrinal differences. This approach interprets Jesus and Muhammad "in the liberative process that makes human history eschatologically dynamic."[79] The second question concerns what this proposal implies for the Muslim belief in the finality of Muhammad. Kerr accepts Muhammad's normativity for Muslims and yet interprets him on the eschatological plane of the "already" but "not yet" of Christian salvation history. This falls well short, then, of a confessional adoption of Muhammad as a prophet. And yet it affirms Muhammad's unique prophetic role in the liberative practices of seventh-century Arabs and beyond. Finally, does this proposal imply that Islam is a valid religion? Kerr maintains that "religions are valid to the degree that they consciously and effectively participate in the process of liberative transformation of human society which is the dynamic of God's action in history."[80] Much as in the case of the finality of Muhammad, this proposal falls short of unqualifiedly affirming Islam. Islam is affirmed insofar as it participates in the liberative transformation of the poor and marginalized in society. Kerr finds, then, that liberation theology is the key lens through which Christians should consider the prophethood of Muhammad. Kerr joins Cragg in recognizing fundamental doctrinal differences between Islam and Christianity, but his strategy is to bypass these differences of doctrine and adopt political theology as the avenue by which to engage the question of prophethood.

It is interesting that Kerr, the final figure considered in this group of four, suggests that fruitful work remains to be done in political theology

rather than in the area of dogmas or creeds, which result in only disagreement and conflict. For it was in the groundbreaking dogmatic
claims of Vatican II that we found, in chapter 2, a new openness to
considering the question of Muhammad. It was the very overlapping
web of beliefs that led to the study of this book. Kerr's position is part
of a larger trend in contemporary theology to eschew theoretical issues and focus on more pragmatic—and therefore less contentious—
grounds for dialogue. This trend is a troubling one, for it accepts rather
than challenges a bifurcation between theory and praxis, between what
we believe and how we conduct ourselves in the modern world. Kerr's
work in political theology could be a possible avenue of exploration
but only as a complement to rather than a replacement of the doctrinal
concerns that animate this book.

ACCEPTING MUHAMMAD'S PROPHETHOOD:
CRITICAL ANALYSIS

The Christian scholars examined above have taken up the question of
Muhammad's prophethood in a serious way. Each has offered a qualified affirmative by focusing on Muhammad's moral exemplarity (Watt),
his invocations against idolatry (Küng), his Qur'anic messages (Cragg),
and his political reforms (Kerr). Kerr hopes to find an inroad through
political rather than doctrinal theology. Watt and Küng both view Muhammad through a historical lens rather than a political one, but this has
the same effect as Kerr's work: it avoids the deep theological questions
that I have tried to address in this book. Cragg's approach is the more
literary of the representative thinkers of this chapter, and his analysis
ends up being more suggestive than prescriptive. But in his recognition
of the deep doctrinal differences and in his attempts to take the Qur'anic
messages theologically seriously, his work can be seen as a precursor to
the argument of this book. The theological significance of Muhammad
for Christians remains, then, an unanswered question.

We might find that liturgical theology offers a fruitful way to move
the conversation forward, for it is in liturgy that we embody what we
believe, where our actions reflect what we hold most dear. We might

find that "Muhammad as liturgical prophet" provides a way forward. Marion Holmes Katz notes in her *Prayer in Islamic Thought and Practice* (2013) that Christians from the thirteenth through the eighteenth centuries who came into contact with Muslims were regularly impressed by their prayer practices, both *salāt* (the canonical prayers performed five times daily) and *duʾāʾ* (supplication). Even the word "read" or "recite" comes from the Semitic root of the word "Qurʾan." Qurʾan means "recitation" in a secondary sense, as in "a sacred text that is recited." This is the same meaning as that of the Syriac word that has the same structure: *qeryānā*. This Syriac term signifies the ritual readings of the office or Mass in the Maronite rite. In other words, it signifies the sacred texts to be read or recited in the Christian tradition.[81] If we turn back to Thomas, we can recall that he explicitly mentions divine worship as a practice that benefits from prophetic guidance.[82] "Muhammad as liturgical prophet," then, is a possible avenue for future investigation. But even here, liturgy embodies in practice what we hold dear in doctrine. The work of this book has been to prepare the theological grounds for considering the possibility of Muhammad's prophethood in Christian terms. Whatever avenue one chooses to embark upon to address the prophetic role of Muhammad must begin from a Christian theology of prophecy. This book is an attempt to provide such a theology and thus offer a launch pad for such an investigation.

Muhammad's Prophethood — Rejecting the Title

In reviewing Christian theologians who took up the question "Is Muhammad a prophet?" and answered in the qualified affirmative, we noted how their conclusions were shaped by theological commitments and how their arguments differ from the one constructed in this book. We will now address two representative theologians who have taken up this question but answered in the negative. We investigate why associating the term "prophet" with Muhammad can be so problematic for Christian theology and address these concerns. Two theologians who have both worked in Muslim-majority countries, whose theology has been shaped by this encounter but who ultimately reject the title "prophet" for Muhammad are Christian Troll, S.J., and Jacques Jomier, O.P.

Christian Troll was honorary professor for the study of Islam and Christian-Muslim Relations at the Philosophisch-Theologische Hochschule St. Georgen in Frankfurt, Germany. Before moving back to Germany, he was a professor at the Vidyajyoti Institute of Religious Studies in Delhi, a senior lecturer at the Center for the Study of Islam and Christian-Muslim Relations in Birmingham, and a Professor of Islamic Institutions at the Pontifical Oriental Institute. For twelve years he worked at the magisterial level of the Catholic Church as a member of the Pontifical Commission for Religious Relations with Muslims in the Pontifical Council for Interreligious Dialogue (PCID). Jacques Jomier was a theology professor in seminaries in Egypt, Iraq, and Nigeria and in the former republic of Zaire, now the Democratic Republic of the Congo, and was one of the founders of the Dominican Institute of Oriental Studies (IDEO) in Cairo. He was a member of the Catholic Institute in Toulouse and served as a consultant to the Vatican Secretariat for Non-Christians. I will examine what animates their reluctance to embrace the prophethood of Muhammad.

Since to Muslim ears a Christian assent to Muhammad as a prophet inevitably means that the Christian has in fact *become a Muslim*, both Troll and Jomier reject the title "prophet." A belief in the prophecy of Muhammad is a belief in all that Islam teaches, including its anti-Christian elements.[83] Islam teaches that Muhammad's recitations are final and universal. A Christian could never accept that claim without ceasing to be a Christian. Particularly problematic is the fact that assenting to Muhammad replaces Jesus's universality with that of Muhammad. Jesus becomes the forerunner, speaking to particular people at a particular time. A Muslim understanding of Muhammad, then, cannot be agreed to by Christians and cannot serve as a meeting place for people of both faiths.[84]

Troll and Jomier analyze the work of some of the theologians discussed above who argued that it might be possible to acknowledge Muhammad as a prophet. These theologians emphasize the "powerful prophetic experience" of Muhammad.[85] But Troll argues that the term "prophet" takes on a third meaning in these theologians' works, different from the one found in either the Bible or the Qur'an. Troll asks whether these theologians are suggesting an "unconditional and comprehensive obedience to the prophet and his teachings" or whether they leave it to individuals to choose between some of the prophet's teachings while objecting to others (he has Hans Küng's work in mind here).[86] Troll accepts that it is plausible to argue that, fundamentally speaking, the Qur'an does not contradict the Christian faith, and where it does, it condemns distorted versions of Christianity, which are also rejected by orthodox Christians (one assumes he means the attack on "tritheism" and the like, although he does not mention these specifically). Troll also accepts that according to a Christian understanding of prophecy, a message can be truly prophetic and yet contain theologically questionable aspects. He ultimately concludes, however, that Muslims would and have reacted negatively to such a redefinition of prophecy, which resembles nothing of the thick theological claims they assume in the term "prophet." He recalls the second Cordoba Colloquium in March of 1977, where a Christian scholar, Gregorio Ruiz González, suggested that if one understood by "prophet" someone gifted with unusual insight and intuition, especially concerning specific social contexts, one might include Muhammad. González identified Karl Marx among the line of "prophets" understood by this definition. Needless to say, many Muslims at the meeting were offended by this proposal and quickly dismissed it.[87] Ultimately, Troll concludes that "from the Muslim perspective, Christians who say that Muhammad is a prophet but do not become Muslims either do not know their own [Christian] faith or are merely playing games."[88]

Troll concedes, however, that while ascribing the term "prophet" to Muhammad is beyond the bounds of Christianity, one should recognize Muhammad's personality, his historic role as religious founder, and his continued role in the devotional life of Muslims.[89] Faithful Christians can choose whether to "dismiss" Muhammad's life and teaching or whether, "in a most impressive manner, these in fact bring to light essential elements of divine truth that are, from the Christian perspective, accessible to human reason and compatible with faith in the person and teaching of Jesus Christ."[90] Note here that Christians can learn from Muslims what they could otherwise learn through the use of their own reason. According to traditional Christian theology, these might include that God is, that God is one, and that God has other attributes that would later, through the light of faith, be applied to the Trinitarian God.

One of the main stumbling blocks to embracing the prophethood of Muhammad has to do with his use of military and political violence, understood theologically as sanctioned against those who rejected his divine message. Troll recognizes the Christian admission of Elijah, for example, as a prophet, despite his use of force, but concludes, "The use of force in the name of God by earlier prophets is thus relativized and stripped of any normative or exemplary significance for Christian thinking and practice."[91] In the end, the prophethood of Muhammad loses its claim to truth and righteousness because of his and his early followers' use of force.

Troll also questions whether Christians can agree to Islam's claim to finality when it appears "imperfect" and "incomplete" when examined by the light of the revelation of Christ. The Islamic categories of "education" and "command" capture only a small part of divine sovereignty. In fact, it is biblical prophets who testify to a much wider vision of divinity. At the end of the day, "there is more to the greatness of God than overcoming polytheism."[92] Troll admits that Muhammad was an "outstanding religio-political figure" but that Christians cannot view Muhammad as a prophet without denying their own faith.[93]

By the time Troll published *Muslims Ask, Christians Answer* (German edition 2003, English translation 2012), he seems to have changed his approach to the question of Muhammad. After summarizing magisterial and other authoritative statements from the Catholic Church, he concludes that these documents encourage Christians to acknowledge both the religious and the ethical values in Muslim belief and practice without at the same time denying any of the essentials of the Christian faith. He concludes, "The way can therefore be open for Christians to recognize in the Qur'an a word from God and in the mission of Muhammad *something prophetic*" (emphasis mine).[94] He adds that the fact that Christians affirm the fullness of revelation in Jesus does not prevent them from recognizing that "God has also made himself known to humanity elsewhere, both before and after

Jesus"; with respect to Muslim belief in particular, "it is possible to acknowledge that the Qur'an contains a word of God, and not only for Muslims, but for all people, and also for me personally."[95] Troll even concludes that the Qur'an "was sent by God to proclaim an essential aspect of the truth, namely the oneness and transcendence of God."[96] Remember, however, that according to traditional Catholic theology these attributes of God, unicity and transcendence, can be known through natural reason.

Troll sets a limit, though, in citing Jacques Jomier, who suggests that Muhammad be referred to as a *guide reformiste* rather than a prophet because it would be "somewhat confusing" to apply the term "prophet" to Muhammad, both from the perspective of Christianity and from an understanding of the Islamic sense of the term. Troll rejects the term "prophet" here in an absolute or strict sense, since it refers to persons who, when speaking prophetically, are "all endowed with divine authority and should be universally obeyed."[97] Since a Christian's faith prohibits her from unreservedly heeding Muhammad's call and, in fact, such heeding would turn her into a Muslim, a Christian cannot embrace the prophecy of Muhammad in a universal sense. Troll concludes that "Christians can use the title 'prophet' with reference to Muhammad only with certain limitations; in other words, they cannot accept everything that this prophet says, but rather will accept some things and reject others."[98] But he then recognizes that this use would be entirely unacceptable to Muslims. In a religious and theological sense, only the prophets of the biblical tradition should be called such; "the title 'prophet' should therefore not be used of Muhammad by Christians; if it is used it would be in a very limited sense which is unacceptable to Muslim faith."[99] Ultimately, Troll shies away from the initial openness to the term "prophet" and decides that Christians should (1) acknowledge the truths that lie within Islam, (2) recognize the spirituality of Muslims, and (3) identify Muhammad as a "religious and political genius."[100] Troll acknowledges God's grace at work in Islam, but says that ultimately it should be considered as an attempt at a radical reform of Judaism and Christianity, "but so radical as to involve the distorting of the essential aspects of both of these traditions."[101] Islam could then be compared to other reform movements in human history. While he does not explicitly mention examples, one imagines that Troll is thinking here of the Protestant Reformation.

Jomier contrasts what it costs a Muslim to proclaim Jesus a prophet and what it costs a Christian to recognize Muhammad as a prophet. For the Muslim, Jesus's prophecy supports Muhammad's role as the seal of the prophets. This is, in fact, Jesus's role in the Qur'an. So it does not cost the Muslim anything, theologically speaking, to recognize Jesus as a prophet, and she has Qur'anic warrant for doing so. In contrast to this case, however, a Christian would have to deny her own faith in order to accept the prophecy of Muhammad in the strict sense.[102] Jomier agrees with Troll in recognizing Muhammad as an exceptional religious figure, but draws the line, along with Troll, at recognizing him as a prophet. To accept Muhammad as a prophet would be to put one's Christian faith at risk. He also shares with Troll the conviction that to Muslim ears a Christian's recognition of the prophethood of Muhammad is an act of conversion. Many Muslims have argued that "if a Christian says that Muhammad is a prophet and does not become a Muslim, either he does not know his religion or he is a hypocrite."[103]

Jomier is, again, in agreement with Troll in ascribing to Muhammad the title of "great politician" and "religious genius."[104] He finds that Christians, when considering the possible truth of the Qur'anic message, should be governed by Galatians 1:8: "But even if we or an angel from heaven should preach to you a gospel contrary to the one we preached to you, let him be accursed." But he tempers this claim by assuring the reader that Islam contains "great intuitions which are profoundly true," intuitions that Christians can sometimes forget.[105] Jomier also concurs that we should think of Islam in terms of a reform movement rather than a prophetic one. He leans on twentieth-century British historian Arnold Toynbee: "'Islam, like Communism, succeeded to the degree that it claimed to be reforming the abuses which had crept into the Christianity of the time. And the success of Islam from the beginning shows to be reforming an orthodoxy which does not seem inclined to reform itself.'"[106] Jomier objects to the fact that the "notion of prophet became singularly flexible, was stretched and transformed"[107] to include Muhammad as a prophet.

In the end, Jomier concedes that Christians could use the word "prophet" for Muhammad, but with qualifications, always accepting some aspects of Muhammad's message but rejecting others. But, most importantly, "here the criteria of acceptance is no longer faith but personal judgment."[108] And yet in the end Jomier concludes, "I personally think that in the present instance we have to avoid the word prophet. To use it would entail giving it a limited sense which Muslim faith would not accept."[109] He adds that we are at a stage where we need to invent a new theological category to point to "those who are profoundly religious but who are in radical opposition to existing official frameworks, and who are rebelling against forms of Christianity which have either become fossilized or are caught up in cultural or national questions."[110] He interprets Islam as the result of a group of "rebels" who let a part of the Christian message get through while rejecting other aspects, which might have occurred "in accordance with the will of God, given the circumstances and the situation of the time."[111]

Both Troll and Jomier engage the question of Muhammad's prophecy theologically, and both come close to a qualified acceptance of Muhammad's prophetic role, but at the end of the day, each decides against such acceptance. Fundamentally, this decision arises from a concern that Muslims would interpret a Christian affirmation of Muhammad's prophecy in a way that is inimical to central Christian beliefs, and a belief that accepting the prophethood of Muhammad inevitably means rejecting fundamental claims of Christianity.

We are left, finally, with the problem that the openness to Muhammad's prophethood observed in the first four thinkers of this chapter sidesteps significant theological questions. When those questions are addressed head-on by theologians who work *ex corde ecclesiae*, the openness turns into an understandable reserve. Is there a way beyond this impasse? Answering this question will become the work of the final chapter. Let us remember that the Church was criticized for being silent about Muhammad during Vatican II. This question needs addressing. But it can be encountered only in deeply Christian theological terms. It does no good to respond to this Muslim criticism by sidestepping the

Christian worldview. The minute one does this, one certainly ceases to be Christian. Intereligious dialogue assumes that each participant is rooted in a tradition of belief and practice; pretending to suspend that belief and practice gets us nowhere. Both Troll and Jomier encounter Muslims' belief and practice in thick Christian theological terms in admirable ways. And yet, it has been the argument of this book that Christians could do more than understand Muhammad as a *guide reformiste*. Surely, when a Muslim calls Jesus a "prophet," she does so with reverence, of course, but with Muslim reverence. She does not mean what a Christian means when she uses that term about Jesus, and yet there is an overlapping sense here of what "prophecy" means to both of them. Theologically significant terms like "prophecy" enjoy multiple layers of meaning that can be mined for the purposes of interreligious dialogue. We turn, then, to this final piece of the argument in chapter 6.

CHAPTER SIX

Closing Argument

In this concluding chapter we unpack how analogical reasoning could help move us through the impasse of either rejecting the possibility of Muhammad's prophethood out of hand or accepting it on terms no orthodox believer—Christian or Muslim—would embrace. If we turn back to Thomas, we find a multilayered understanding of Christian prophecy, such that what Muhammad heard and communicated in seventh-century Arabia in principle could fall under the term "prophecy," understood in its most expansive sense. In the strictest understanding of prophecy, the person receives knowledge or images beyond the reaches of human reason and makes a judgment about that knowledge or those images. But Thomas suggests that the experience of prophecy encompasses a wide range of instances documented in Scripture, such that the term already enjoys a certain elasticity within the scriptural text. Only in some cases does the person enjoy the full office of prophet. Thomas's taxonomy seeks to capture this wide range. It has been the work of this book to suggest that his understanding of prophecy, married to the doctrinal claims made at Vatican II about the overlapping web of beliefs between Christians and Muslims, should open up the theoretical possibility that Muhammad spoke prophetically. For Christians, Muhammad did not enjoy the full office of prophet in the way that John the Baptist did, but he could have participated in the prophetic experience in the way of Caiaphas or the Roman soldiers. At times he could even have spoken prophetically as did Solomon, whose intellect was strengthened to understand things otherwise known through natural reason. This theoretical openness need not resolve in advance whether what Muhammad heard from the angel Gabriel could have been understood through natural reason or whether it needed the help of divine grace. Thomas's understanding of prophecy included both of these possibilities. Given that prophetic knowledge is transitory and not habitual, Muhammad could have experienced prophetic knowledge in different ways at different times.

Here prophecy is understood analogically, with the outer meanings related to but distinct from the primary meaning of prophecy. It might be that traditionally minded Christians tend toward univocal language, such that our religious categories cannot reach beyond our ecclesial walls. Liberally minded Christians, on the other hand, jump to equivocal language, understanding our categories to be fundamentally different, but the differences are erased ultimately in the search for peace among religions. Thomas himself invoked analogical reasoning in his analysis of prophecy. We might take his lead where he did not himself go into the theology of religious pluralism.

Prophecy and Analogy

Peter commanded the early Christian community to "always be ready to give an explanation to anyone who asks [us] for a reason for [our] hope" (1 Pt. 3:15).[1] He urged his listeners to give an account—in Greek, an *apologion*—for the hope that was in them. Narrating our "apologias" is a primary way to encounter those of other faith traditions.[2] But this encounter cannot stop here. For our conversation to develop, we need to move from apologia to analogia. In apologia we speak words "from" or "out of" our narrative, but in analogia we are taking words "up" from our narrative and seeing how those words cohere in other religious traditions.

Recalling Thomas, univocity and equivocity were the poles within which he crafted an analogical "third way" in medieval Europe. These poles reemerge in our contemporary context as the dual challenges of Christian imperialism, on the one hand, and the incommensurability of faith traditions, on the other. Introducing analogy into the theology of religious pluralism offers us a way to resist the two extremes. It resists the temptation of univocity—forcing the beliefs and practices of other religious traditions into our own Christian terms—or rejecting them if they do not fit—in an act of imperialism. It also resists the temptation to resort to equivocity—maintaining that religious traditions are ultimately irreducible, such that one term holds no purchase across traditions. Instead of becoming mired in the scholarship on the use of analogy in Christian theology,[3] David Burrell, C.S.C., will act as a guide in this constructive proposal. Burrell embodies in practice the intellectual trajectory of his work. His first book, *Analogy and Philosophical Language* (1973), planted seeds that bore fruit years later in his groundbreaking work in comparative theology.[4]

Drawing inspiration from Thomas's understanding of analogy in the area of religious pluralism admittedly involves moving his work into new territory.[5] He used analogy primarily in the arena of divine names. Analogy is invoked here to balance two main commitments: (1) to maintain that God is inconceivable mystery, and (2) to speak truthfully when we make claims about God. Analogy steers a middle course between univocal and equivocal language,[6] each of which is seriously deficient. In univocal language, we reduce God to one creature among others in the universe—and become idolaters in quick turn; in equivocal language, our God-talk becomes mere babble.

Thomas distinguishes between metaphor and analogy to show that while all language is wrapped in human clothing, some ways that we talk about God reach further than others.[7] When we say, "God is good," we understand that goodness applies to God in an utterly perfect way, a way unknown to us. But we believe that goodness in God is related—analogously—to goodness in humans. So our words, while not able to capture the whole meaning of how God is good, capture *something* of what this would mean. If it can even be called a shadow, goodness as we understand it is a pale shadow of how good God is, but even though it has the relationship only of shadow to statue, it nonetheless reflects something true about God, however vaguely or imperfectly. We can never adequately express how the reflection mirrors the statue, but we can have confidence that our speech is not meaningless. Thomas reminds us throughout his writings that while we can apprehend aspects of God, we could never fully comprehend our subject. While heeding pseudo-Dionysius and Rabbi Maimonides' warnings against idolatry, Thomas chose not to follow their tendencies toward agnosticism. Instead, he maintained that the faithful can speak about God in a true, incomplete, and not fully choate way. This speech is always offered against a backdrop of radical difference between creatures and their Creator. Christians must be cautious in their language about God, but they can speak about God from observing His pulse in the world. They must recognize continuously that these claims belie a greater ignorance of the essence of God. While religious claims must be open to further refinement, revision, and even rejection, they are justifiable attempts to make true statements about their subject, God. Whether in ordinary discourse, in religious worship, or in theological examination, Thomas assures Christians that their pursuit is not fruitless, that their proclamations really do signify something true about God. They will never have the last word, but the words they use are meaningful and true. With Burrell, we see that Thomas offered not so much a theory on analogy as a practice of analogical reasoning. Certain terms can be used properly of both God and creatures, although we can never speak adequately of God by using these terms. These terms, however, cannot be univocal. They must be able to reach across "the distinction" between creatures and their Creator without dissolving it.[8]

A theology of religious pluralism must move this theological practice into a secondary sense of analogy, one that recognizes resemblances among religious traditions against the backdrop of radical difference. There is an implicit faith here that some of our words can have purchase across faith traditions, an implicit faith that we are all on a similar quest—not a quest that can be reducible to some common denominator, one that is framed in human terms, with human questions that inevitably reach beyond themselves. The grounding relationship between Creator and creatures that undergirds Thomas's analogical practice reemerges when trying to understand terms in another religious tradition in two ways. In the first, we recognize that all theological language in Abrahamic traditions—whether Jewish, Christian, or Muslim—is grounded in the Creator/creature distinction, however differently each tradition might name that distinction.[9] In the second, each of the three traditions shares certain figures and terms—of which prophecy is one—but understands them in different ways. If each tradition is really naming the incomprehensible mystery that is God, there must be a way to make sense of one another's names, even if the sense we make is limited, partial, and tentative. Metaphysical grounding for theology is shared among the three traditions, and the historical details and religious terms overlap. Christian theological discourse not only has the ability to reach beyond its native territory by speaking analogously about God; it can also reach beyond its ken into other traditions through analogical reasoning. In recognizing the backdrop of difference, it refrains from colonizing terms from the "religious other." In acknowledging similarities, it does not view differences among religious traditions as fundamentally irreducible.

Impressive attempts to negotiate religious difference on a third, objective, rational ground have been tried[10] and found lacking.[11] Instead we opt with Burrell to accept different paths to similar conclusions, where "we can employ the skills learned in our tradition to follow reasoning in another. Traditions, in other words, may indeed be *relative* to one another in ways that can prove mutually fruitful rather than isolating (emphasis in original). Those traditions which prove to be so will be those which avail themselves of human reason in their development, and the patterns of stress and strain in their evolution will display their capacity for exploiting the resources of reason."[12] The negotiating practice here is analogy, for traditions may become mutually illuminating only if they share enough terms to enable reasonable communication. Reason no longer corresponds to a set of beliefs that must be accepted by all before conversation begins. Rather, "*rationality* will then show itself in practices which can be followed and understood by persons operating in similar fashion from different grounding convictions" (emphasis in original).[13] It is the task of the theology of religious pluralism to recognize the patterns of similarities and differences through analogical reasoning. Burrell concludes, "We can hardly appreciate the valence of analogous discourse, and its indispensability in communicating our basic human aspirations, unless we allow ourselves to be challenged by those who hold similar hopes but may express them in ways that differ widely from our own."[14] Analogy is crucial here because religious terms are used in multiple yet ordered ways. Without resulting in a theory of analogy, the practice is ultimately revealed through examples.

Burrell employs the example of a married couple for whom the declaration "I love you" means something related to but radically different from its meanings during the second and twenty-fifth years of their marriage. What changes is the point of reference. They loved each other during their second year, but from the perspective of their twenty-fifth year, their earlier declaration seems like mere pleasantry compared to what they have come to discover over the past twenty-three years: "Their earlier avowal seems so remote from their current paradigm—what they have discovered loving one another to be and to entail—that it seems barely to qualify for inclusion in the notion. Yet a more extended narrative—a life story—should be able to trace those shifts in a sufficiently ordered way to indicate the connections, however dramatic the shifts may have been."[15] No concrete univocal core of meaning exists between the expression of love at the beginning of a marriage and that in its maturity. What changes is the paradigm through which the couple understands the term: "And the story of those shifts—tantamount to a life story—offers sufficient coherence to assure us we are using the same notion. If no such story can be forged, of course, we have sheer ambiguity—just as a variety of viewpoints may never become pluralistic but remain simply diverse."[16] Much as we try to construct a definition of marital love, we will always be caught resorting to ambiguous terms. And so it is in the theology of religious pluralism.

Does analogical reasoning relativize Jesus of Nazareth to some wider criterion of truth? If we turn to Rowan Williams for guidance, we find that invoking Jesus Christ as the measure of truth opens rather than shuts down our considerations of the claims of the religious other: "The identity of Jesus must engage with the worlds of human meaning for them to be meaningful in any other than 'tribal,' limited contexts: the meaning of Jesus is not the container of all other meanings but their test, judgment and catalyst. Jesus does not have to mean everything; his 'universal significance' is a universally crucial question rather than a comprehensive ontological schema."[17] Listening to the seeds of the Word in other faith traditions means we are listening more—not less—attentively, to the words of the Gospel.

While we cannot offer a theory of analogical reasoning, we can point to its patterns of usage. Burrell maintains: "In the measure that we can be aware of using an expression beyond its normal reach, because we have come to experience that term's ability to render our own aspirations at various points of attainment or failure, then we can be said to be using it *properly*. It is of such awareness that analogous usage is born, and in developing that awareness it is warranted" (emphasis in original).[18] In deciding whether another story is coherent or not, we must share something in common to make this decision. Radical cultural differences can certainly pose a barrier here. But when they do not, we use narrative in theological argument initially to recognize the kind of relationship we have to each other and, further, are able to help each other to notice the coherence in our faith stories. The pattern of discussion here is analogical. When Muslims revere Jesus as a prophet, they are not revering him as Christians do, and they are not equating this prophetic role with Muhammad's singular one. I suggest that Christians might come to revere Muhammad as a prophet in a limited and relative sense, not one that Muslims would embrace, but one that Christians nevertheless should consider.[19] Troll and Jomier are right to note that to Muslim ears, this Christian use of "prophet" will not satisfy. But neither will the Muslim reverence of Jesus satisfy the Christian. The fundamental conflict between the two traditions' universal claim remains. And yet the overlapping web of beliefs between the two traditions delineated by the conciliar documents means that we share a meaningful arena of discourse.

The preceding chapters have offered a preliminary argument for a much longer and wider examination of the life and work of Muhammad and theological analysis of the Qur'an. The Church already has in its tradition, however, long-standing patterns and practices of spiritual discernment that could be appealed to in this interreligious context. It also has an ecclesial process of discerning the validity of postcanonical "private revelations." This process might be adapted to the discernment of Muhammad's revelations in seventh-century Arabia.

Excavating a Forgotten Resource:
Private Revelation

Private revelation is a neglected and idiosyncratic category in the Catholic theological tradition, due perhaps to its usual connection to extraordinary events of Marian apparition. It might be considered the area in which the experience of the faithful has had the most marked effect on Church teaching. Popular devotion to Mary throughout the Church's history has led to liturgical celebrations, theological deliberations, and even dogmatic pronouncements. The category of "private revelation" has been developed in the Church, at least in part, to capture at one and the same time the validity of Marian apparitions and their distinctness from the deposit of faith. The *Catechism of the Catholic Church* states: "Throughout the ages, there have been so-called 'private' revelations, some of which have been recognized by the authority of the Church. They do not belong, however, to the deposit of faith. It is not their role to improve or complete Christ's definitive Revelation, but to help live more fully by it in a certain period of history. Guided by the magisterium of the Church, the *sensus fidelium* knows how to discern and welcome in these revelations whatever constitutes an authentic call of Christ or his saints to the Church."[20] The *Catechism* makes clear the ancillary role of private revelation in the life of the Church. An analysis of the theological underpinnings of the term "private revelation" will help us recover a category that acknowledges God's continual revelatory activity in the world while respecting the fulfillment of public revelation with the Christ event. After the synod of bishops met in 2008 to discuss the Word of God, Benedict XVI issued his postsynodal Apostolic Exhortation, *Verbum Domini*, in September of 2010. He took up the issue of private revelation in that document and suggested that it "can introduce new emphases, give rise to new forms of piety, or deepen older ones. *It can have a certain prophetic character* (cf. 1 Th. 5:19–21) and can be a valuable aid for better understanding and living the Gospel at a certain time; consequently it should not be treated lightly" (emphasis mine).[21]

This revelatory activity is held distinct from the traditional deposit of faith. No Catholic is obliged to believe in this or that particular private revelation. Deciding whether an alleged revelation is authentic, however, is a delicate and complicated matter. The Church has a long tradition of principles of discernment on which to draw in order to distinguish true revelations from their false counterparts. These principles exercised in discerning private revelation help the magisterium broaden awareness of the workings of the Holy Spirit. As John Paul II affirmed, "It is the same Spirit who assists the Magisterium and awakens the *sensus fidei.*"[22] To set the preliminary groundwork for a discussion of private revelation outside Christianity, we must first outline the role of such revelation in the life of the Church.

Private revelation arises out of the prophetic element of the Church; it is one of the ways that prophecy takes shape. The theology behind private revelation moves from its theoretical possibility to the concrete documentation of its occurrence. Karl Rahner argues that at the very least private revelation in the Church has to be allowed in principle, for its denial would throw the whole of Christian belief into doubt: "The history of Christianity would be unthinkable without prophetic and visionary elements (in the broadest sense). To try to explain all these things by natural or even abnormal human causes, would be logically to deny that any historical activity of the personal God revealing himself in the Word was possible at all. But this would be to repudiate the character of Christianity as an historical, supernatural, revealed religion."[23] Belief that God became incarnate in a Palestinian Jew at a concrete moment in history means that human ears must be open to encountering God in history, even in unexpected ways. That Jesus of Nazareth fulfilled the messianic expectations of the Hebrew Scriptures certainly attests to the surprising way that God chose to express Himself in history. In Christ we have "God's final and definitive revelation and self-disclosure."[24] Supernatural revelation, then, is essential to Christianity; it is "basic" revelation. But the logic of supernatural revelation leads directly to the possibility of private revelation.

This theoretical openness becomes concrete when we turn to the testimony of Scripture. The Gospels document that before the birth of Christ, God spoke to His people in history.[25] This history of revelation, although incomplete in itself, was preparatory in nature and was

completed by the fullness of revelation in Christ. The Gospels themselves announced John the Baptist, the last of the prophets to predict
Christ's coming and the first to point directly to Christ,[26] and the letters of Paul provide evidence of the movement of the Spirit in the early
Christian community.[27] While revelation received its climax and fulfillment in the coming of Christ, the New Testament documents an
expansion of new charisms and prophecies after His death. Of New
Testament prophets after the death of Christ, Niels Hvidt argues: "The
role of the prophets after Christ is to lead the church to the truth and
fullness of God in Christ, just as it was the role of the Old Testament
prophets to lead God's people to remain faithful to the revelation God
has conferred on Moses. Just as the Old Testament prophets fought to
keep God's people faithful to the covenant, so now the prophets in the
New Testament, and in Christ's church, are called to keep believers
faithful to the covenant of the New Testament, sealed with the blood
of the Lamb."[28] The New Testament suggests that prophecy will be a
permanent feature of the life of the Church.

Ongoing miracles, interventions, and revelations have typically
been used as evidence of such prophecy in the Church, reflecting an
assumption that they are a permanent part of it. Hans Küng, commenting on *Lumen Gentium*, argues for an ongoing charismatic structure to the Church that is not limited to a particular group of persons
but rather is widely shared in the Church: "All this implies also that
[the charismata] are not a thing of the past (possible and real only in
the early Church), but eminently contemporary and actual; they do
not hover on the periphery of the Church but are eminently central
and essential to it. In this sense one should speak of a *charismatic structure of the Church* which embraces and goes beyond the structure of
government" (emphasis in original).[29] Recognizing private revelation
is one way that the Church affirms ongoing divine manifestations in
history, even those since the definitive and normative Christ event.
These revelations have a different character and status in the Church,
to be sure, but the logic of the incarnation—that God reveals Himself
in history—leads directly to the possibility of postbiblical revelation.
This possibility falls within the prophetic element of the Church and
includes instances of private revelation. I have argued in this book that

much as the prior Israelite and subsequent Christian revelations attested to in Scripture, non-Christian "private revelations" or divine encounters (1) do not modify Christian revelation but (2) derive their validity from Christ in some way and (3) provide a creative avenue for deepening our understanding of basic revelation.

So the question of the character and status of private revelation arises. Thomas Aquinas understood prophecy as a kind of knowledge that divine revelation impresses on the prophet's intellect under the form of teaching.[30] Instances of private revelation fall within this prophetic or charismatic element in the Church, for they reflect an encounter with God or a messenger of God that, while sometimes ineffable, often presents a message to the faithful.[31] The recipients of these revelations, much like the prophets of the Hebrew Scriptures, often express surprise and hesitation at being chosen. While theologians regularly cite Aquinas in affirming that the goal of prophecy is to direct human activity,[32] Hvidt argues that prophecy is also directed toward understanding Christian revelation more adequately: "Christian prophecy is not revelation on par with the Bible, but this does not mean that it cannot serve as verification of and support for revelation. Postcanonical Christian prophecy can indeed serve to elucidate points of Scripture that are not clear or that Scripture contains in an implicit way only, and as such it can and has indeed played a very important role in the correction and actualization of our understanding of revelation."[33] In Church history, prophecy was linked with predicting future events. Bernard McGinn, however, finds that in early medieval Christianity the "broadest and most significant function of prophecy . . . was its identification with the spiritual interpretation of the Bible and preaching."[34]

A word should be said about what is both private and revelatory about private revelations. The term "private" is misleading. Revelations, while usually received by individual persons, nevertheless often involve a message to the Church as a whole. The term "private" stresses the fact that Catholics are not obliged to believe in these revelations. In fact, Benedict XIV's eighteenth-century *De servorum Dei* suggests that no Catholic is obliged to believe occurrences of this sort: "The approval that the Church gives to a private revelation is simply a permission, based on a careful examination, to allow the revelation to be

promulgated for the instruction and profit of the faithful."[35] Rahner
prefers the terminology of "prophetic visions." Laurent Volken, Avery
Dulles, Pierre Adnès, and Augustinus Suh prefer the term "particular"
or "special" revelation.[36] Hvidt opts for "prophetic revelations," as it
underscores the fact that the function of postapostolic revelations is
similar to that of biblical prophecy: "This term marks the difference
between the postapostolic revelations and the *revelatio publica*. It indicates not only that such revelations are the direct result of divine intervention, but that they actually fulfill the function in the church of
communicating an intelligible message to the congregation and that it
has prophetic purpose."[37] Each of the theologians cited above argues
for a change in terminology because each seeks to raise the status
of private revelations and to acknowledge their legitimate function in
the lives of the faithful and the Church at large. Their arguments are
largely persuasive.

But preserving the terminology of "private revelation" also has
advantages. It is, as Dulles asserts, the term that has gained "wider cur-
rency,"[38] but it also preserves an important continuity with other
terms in the Church, such as "private mass" or "private prayer." These
terms also affect the whole Church and are in some important ways
not private. But the terms make sense only in relationship to the in-
verse terms, "communal mass" and "communal prayer." It is not that
private prayer or private masses do not affect the whole Church in a
real way; it is, rather, that they need to be distinguished from their
communal counterparts with respect to their role in the life of the
Church. The communal experience of mass and prayer is at the center;
private mass and private prayer are rooted in that center. Private revelation is also rooted in the wider revelation of the Church. The Israelite prophetic tradition was preparatory to the revelation of Christ;
postbiblical private revelations ultimately derive their meaning from
the Christ event. Both, however, retain their own intrinsic value for
ordering individual Christians and their communities. Maintaining the
terminology of "private revelation" has an important advantage for
the argument of this book. Since "private revelation" accentuates its
distinction from the deposit of the faith, it is easier to stretch this term
to capture the encounter between non-Christians and God.

What, then, is properly revelatory in private revelations? Much work has been done since the 1950s and 1960s in the theology of revelation. Two significant markers of this development include (1) as noted in chapter 2, the movement away from revelation as propositional disclosure of truths and toward revelation as a dynamic encounter between persons[39] and (2) the recognition of the relationship between the history of revelation and that of salvation. Hvidt documents the first marker in the shift that occurred "from a rather propositional to a more dynamic understanding of revelation that sees revelation as the communication of God's life-reality to his church, a reality that encompasses cognitive aspects while remaining continuously in need of vivification in order to become a powerful expression of God's image in every new historical context."[40] Rahner, in asserting that revelation closed with the cross, marks the shift from revelation conceived of as a set of propositions to revelation conceived of as a dynamic reality into which the faithful are invited. He also recognizes the second marker of revelation as occurring against the backdrop of eschatological expectations. The cross represents God's irrevocable promise to us, and it is God's final word, to which nothing more can be added. But "within this final word history also continues as God's revelation—the history that we usually describe as history of the Church and history of faith, which is the history of this final word of God and thus, rightly understood, can also continue to be described as history of revelation."[41] Dulles places his discussion of revelation within the plan of salvation history, for he acknowledges that revelation still awaits the full manifestation of Jesus Christ at the end of time: "Revelation, therefore, either coincides with the end of history or anticipates that end. Within time, revelation is given only under the form of promise or anticipation of a fuller revelation yet to be given."[42] Instances of private revelation fall within this pattern of already-but-not-yet, helping Christians to more adequately understand and live out what has already been given to them in fuller anticipation of the encounter with Christ that is yet to come at the end of time.

Regardless of the terminological issue—whether we call these revelations "private," "special," or "prophetic"—we are naming a postbiblical revelatory experience that is rooted in the Christ event.

While that experience is secondary, subsequent to biblical revelation, it is properly ordered to the revelation found in Christ and is one possible expression of the prophetic or charismatic element of Church life. This postbiblical revelatory experience could be stretched to the theology of religious pluralism. Stretching theological terms to fit the context of radical religious pluralism is urgent today, as it helps us answer the call of *Nostra Aetate*. We stretch and adapt traditional terms both to affirm confidently our own tradition and to recognize the truth and holiness of other traditions.

Can this category be applied in a non-Christian context as a way to acknowledge revelatory activity that both draws its source from the cross and anticipates the final coming of Christ? The history of revelation in which Christians are invited to participate also presents an invitation beyond the boundaries of the visible Church. In principle, there is no reason why the category of private revelation cannot be expanded to non-Christian encounters with God. As far back as 1937, Yves Congar wrote a landmark article on private revelations in which he included non-Christians: "Private revelations are commonly understood as those revelations in which a soul, *be it Christian or not*, is the subject of God on a personal or private level, and not as an initiator or a doctor of the universal religion in which God works the salvation of humanity" (emphasis mine).[43] This understanding of private revelation might be too individualistic, but it affirms that the one who receives the divine message need not be Christian. The authenticity of the divine-human encounter is acknowledged even in non-Christian contexts and need not, but may be, affirmed by Catholics.

What should the Christian community's response be to the claim of private revelation? What level of faith commitment does the claim expect of the individual believer and the wider community? Here again, practices of discernment within the Church that have been applied to Christian private revelation can be adapted to our contemporary context of religious pluralism. A medieval distinction emerged in Scholastic theology among *fides humana*, *fides divina*, and *fides catholica* that influenced the formulations of the ecclesial magisterium.[44] Arguments for the faith based on human reason are to be believed by *fides humana*. Objects immediately revealed are to be believed with *fides divina*, as the belief due them is based on the authority of God, who reveals them. Of these, those proclaimed by the Church to form the deposit of faith are to be believed by *fides catholica*. These are fundamental truths of Scripture and tradition, rooted in the Church's experience before the death of the last apostle. There is general theological consensus on what comprises *fides catholica*.

When it comes to private revelations that have occurred since the death of the last apostle, however, there is a range of theological opinion. The minimalists, who are hesitant to ask the faithful to believe any particular instance of private revelation, maintain that occurrences of private revelation call forth belief only by *fides humana*.[45] This is the view taken by modern Thomists and pointedly adopted by Congar.[46] It is also the view upheld in magisterial documents but not necessarily in individual papal pronouncements regarding certain apparitions.[47] The maximalists, who are more willing to allow the faithful to believe particular instances of private revelation, counter that the substance of the truth itself encountered in private revelation is rooted in the same truth as the deposit of faith. Consequently, it may be believed by *fides divina*. In this view, the fact of the revelation is to be believed only with *fides humana*, but the actual content of the revelation is to be believed with *fides divina*.[48] Magisterial documents side with the minimalists in affirming that a person may withhold belief in these revelations, provided she does so with "due modesty, not without reason, and without contempt."[49] Commenting on the apparitions at Lourdes and La Salette, Pope Pius IX stated that the "Apostolic See has neither approved nor condemned such apparitions or revelations but merely permits Catholics to believe in them—where they have the support of credible witness and documents—with a merely human faith [*fide solum humana*]."[50] Pope Pius X reaffirmed this principle in his encyclical *Pascendi dominici gregis* on the Modernist controversy when addressing how to manage the veneration of sacred relics: "In passing judgment on pious traditions be it always borne in mind that in this matter the Church uses the greatest prudence, and that she does not allow traditions of this kind to be narrated in books except with the utmost caution and with the insertion of the declaration imposed by Urban VIII, and even then she does not guarantee the truth of the fact narrated; the Church merely does not prohibit belief, unless human arguments for belief are wanting."[51] The range of theological opinions regarding whether private revelations should be believed with *fides divina* or *fides humana* could arise from the fact that private revelations are a complex reality. It is prudent for the Church to err on the side of *fides humana* in its magisterial documents. But it is also possible that a certain instance of private revelation, given its particular shape and circumstances, calls forth a deeper faith commitment on the part of both the recipient and the wider Christian community.

In developing norms for judging apparitions and private revelations, the Church draws on longstanding practices of spiritual discernment. The canonical norms date back to the 1978 CDF document "Norms . . . on the Manner of Proceeding in Judging Alleged Apparitions and Revelations."[52] Arising out of a particular historical context, the norms followed upon a noteworthy relaxation of the prohibitions and censures of publications dealing with apparitions and private revelations.[53] The rise of mass media enabled news of apparitions to spread quickly among the faithful, and the ease of travel enabled journeys to pilgrimage sites. The norms outline a series of criteria to help ecclesiastical authorities discern the validity of claims of private revelations and respond to them quickly and effectively.

The fact that private revelations are received by humans and communicated by human means introduces the possibility of multiple errors. A given private revelation might be authentic, but it could also be entangled in errors resulting from its reception and transmission.[54] Even a canonized saint can distort a revelation approved by the Church. Errors that might find their way into a given private revelation do not automatically invalidate the revelation as a whole. Conversely, that a given revelation proves true (for example, in the case of a historical prediction) does not in itself mean that the revelation was divine in nature.[55]

In the history of Marian apparitions, a dilemma arises between the urgency of the messages received from the Blessed Mother and the prudence required by the Church in evaluating these apparitions. Discernment about Marian apparitions is contested, marked by a push and pull between the faithful who believe in the apparitions and the ecclesial authorities who urge prudence.[56] One should expect this same tension to arise, then, when trying to stretch the category of private revelation to non-Christian revelations.

The process of discernment, while using Christian dogma as its main guide, opens the possibility that the Qur'anic message clarifies neglected aspects of the Christians tradition. Much as David Burrell finds that robust Jewish and Muslim doctrines of creation can highlight for Christians our own tendency to let the doctrine of atonement overshadow the doctrine of Creation, the argument of this book suggests that Christians should be open to the possibility that the Qur'an can clarify our own Christian beliefs and practices.[57] This openness does not mean that Christians will or should adopt the Qur'an as revelatory as a whole, but rather that passages in the Qur'an could help Christians clarify their own faith on particular issues. Such judgments can occur only in the particular. So, for example, what Daniel Madigan asserts about *Nostra Aetate* and other religions would in general also hold for Christian openness to the Qur'an in particular:

> Perhaps, then, the question about means and structures, on which *Nostra Aetate* did not offer an explicit opinion, needs to be rephrased. Instead of asking, "Is this religion a structure or vehicle or way of salvation?" should we not rather ask, "Are there elements in this religion that God appears to be using to save people?" Thus there is no single, *a priori* answer to the question of how salvific other religions are. We can only make an *a posteriori* judgement, based on an observation of the fruits of the Spirit and the distinguishing marks of the Kingdom in the followers of that particular religion. Such an *a posteriori* judgement cannot or need not be made about the whole religion, but rather about individual elements.[58]

The way the Church understands the unusual category of private revelation provides a fruitful avenue for this kind of openness. The theology of private revelation outlined above coheres naturally with Thomas Aquinas's understanding of prophecy. "Prophecy" names a complex array of encounters with God. Some instances partake in part of the prophetic experiences, while others more fully reflect what it means to prophesy. Sometimes a prophet mixes elements of mistaken human judgment with true prophetic revelation. Prophecies could be received about things that human reason could otherwise come to understand or about things known only through the assistance of divine grace. Judging whether a particular prophecy is true can be done only on an *ad hoc* basis. As a result, particular passages in the Qur'an could be explored without having to make any claims about the book as a whole. The argument of this book concludes with an invitation to read the Qur'an and take it theologically seriously, as it could very well contain messages of prophetic import. The preceding chapters have established the groundwork for such an invitation.[59]

These chapters have offered theological warrant from the heart of one religious tradition to examine the doctrines, patterns, and practices of another without ignoring one's home territory. As Peter Ochs says of scriptural reasoning, we "seek after God's word in our own way" after having passed through dialogue and friendship with the religious other.[60] The method has been one of digging deep within one's own tradition and bringing to light two neglected categories—that of Thomas Aquinas on prophecy and that of twentieth-century theology on private revelation—and marrying them to the doctrinal claims made at Vatican II. This work opens up the theoretical possibility that Muhammad was a religious prophet. It might be that it is prudent for the Church to remain at the level of theoretical openness in its official documents. But this should not keep individual Christians from accepting the invitation of this book to mine the Qur'an for nuggets of the Word.

NOTES

CHAPTER ONE. Setting the Stage

1. Huntington, *The Clash of Civilizations*.

2. This is, of course, advice that his critics have noted that he would do well to heed.

3. For criticism from quantitative studies, see Fox, "Paradigm Lost," 428–57. From cultural criticism, see Said, "The Clash of Ignorance." From philosophy, see Sen, *Identity and Violence*. From a public policy perspective, see Mahbubani and Summers, "The Fusion of Civilizations." In 2013, *Foreign Affairs* published an e-book to celebrate Huntington's original essay (which had become a book by the same name) by subsequently republishing it along with several critical essays and Huntington's response to his critics. See https://www.foreignaffairs.com/.

4. Buckley, *Denying and Disclosing God*, 138.

5. Lilla, "The Politics of God."

6. See Jenkins, *The New Faces of Christianity*, and his *God's Continent*. See also Cox, *The Market as God*.

7. Lilla, *The Stillborn God*, 217. For an incisive criticism of Lilla's argument and an alternative account of the history of the relationship between Christian political theology and modern liberalism, see Philpott, "Political Theology and Liberal Democracy."

8. Lilla, *The Stillborn God*, 260.

9. Lilla, "The Truth About [sic] Our Libertarian Age."

10. For a different historical approach that accentuates Christianity's underappreciated role in the development of basic human rights and freedoms from antiquity to the modern world, see the two-volume collection edited by Shah and Hertzke, *Christianity and Freedom*.

11. Cavanaugh, "Religious Violence as Modern Myth," 487. Cavanaugh's book has elicited much discussion and criticism in the years since its publication. The volume of *Political Theology* cited here is devoted to a discussion of the book, including this article, where Cavanaugh responds to some of his critics.

12. Hart, *Atheist Delusions*, 14.

13. Of the religious wars of the sixteenth and seventeenth centuries, Hart observes that "they inaugurated a new age of nationalist strife and state violence, prosecuted on a scale and with a degree of ferocity without any precedent in medieval history," and that, in fact, "far from the secular nation state rescuing Western humanity from the chaos and butchery of sectarian strife, those wars were the birth pangs of the modern state and its limitless license to murder" (*Atheist Delusions*, 89).

14. Rejecting a modern understanding of religion as a set of universal norms is not to deny that religion was understood by many pre-modern Christian thinkers, such as Augustine, Cicero, and Tertullian, to be a basic transhistorical, transcultural human good. See Smith, *Religion*.

15. Toft, Philpott, and Shah, *God's Century*, 3.

16. Manent, *Beyond Radical Secularism*, 105.

17. The methodology of this book is analogous to Daniel Philpott's approach in his *Just and Unjust Peace*, 18–22, of "rooted reason," in which participants in a dialogue are able to bring to the table the full range and depth of their beliefs.

18. From the eighth century, John of Damascus introduced Islam as the forerunner of the antichrist in his *Writings*. For an account of medieval interpretations of Islam, see Tolan, *Saracens*. See also Southern, *Western Views of Islam in the Middle Ages*. For an overview of Western misunderstandings of Islam from the Crusades onward, see Daniel, *Islam and the West*. For a recent insightful account of a "European Muhammad," where Muhammad emerges as a "mirror" for European hopes, fears, and ambitions such that the portrayals of him over the centuries in Europe are not actually about Islam but instead reflect an intra-Christian polemic, see Tolan, *Mahomet l'Européen*.

19. Lehner, *The Catholic Enlightenment*, 15.

20. Anawati, "Excursus on Islam," 154.

21. Some Eastern Christian polemicists were willing to call Muhammad a local prophet (but not a universal prophet) precisely because he succeeded in convincing the Arabs to accept monotheism. The anti-Islamic arguments of Eastern Christians such as those in the *Risala ila al-Muslimin* or those of Bishop Paul of Antioch (twelfth century) include the following affirmation of Muhammad's localized prophethood: "We know that he was not sent to us, but to the Arabs of the Jahiliyya of whom he said that there had come to them no warner before him. We know that he did not obligate us to follow him because there had come to us before him prophets who had preached and warned us in our own languages." Bishop Paul of Antioch, quoted in Michel, *A Muslim Theologian's Response to Christianity*, 88. I am grateful to Rita George-Tvrtkovic for pointing me to this source.

22. While the argument of this book specifically engages the Muslim critique at Vatican II that the Catholic Church did not address the question of Muhammad's prophecy in an explicit way, there is, admittedly, work to be done on how the concept of Christian prophecy relates to a Jewish understanding of prophecy. But that question lies outside the scope of the present argument.

23. In December of 2016 the Danish Medical Association recommended ending the practice of male circumcision for boys, a move that would target Muslim and Jewish communities. See Danish Medical Association (laeger.dk), "Lægeforeningen."

24. Madigan, "Jesus and Muhammad," 90.

25. Of particular note here is the development of the Secretariat for Non-Christians (1964), renamed the Pontifical Council for Inter-religious Dialogue in 1988. Within the several important documents published by this council, one must highlight *Guidelines for Dialogue between Christians and Muslims* (1981), *Dialogue and Mission* (1984), and *Dialogue and Proclamation* (1991). Together, these three documents place dialogue within the mission of the church alongside proclamation, seeing them both as necessary, indispensable elements of the church's work. For a helpful history of the Holy See's developments on inter-religious dialogue since the promulgation of *NA* (1965), see Cassidy, *Ecumenism and Interreligious Dialogue*, 125–264. For an overview of the development of the declaration, see the five-volume *History of Vatican II*, ed. Alberigo and Komonchak, esp. vol. 4, 135–64 and 546–59, and vol. 5, 211–20.

26. For a brief and well-documented presentation of the complexity of the reception of Vatican II into the life of the Church, see Faggioli, *Vatican II*. The most expansive efforts in Vatican II scholarship include Vorgrimler, *Commentary on the Documents of Vatican II*, and Hünermann and Hilberath, *Herder theologischer Kommentar zum zweiten Vatikanischen Konzil*. On the history of the development of the documents, Giuseppe Alberigo and his collaborators at the Fondazione per le Scienze Religiose compiled a five-volume *History of Vatican II*. Recent scholarship that follows that general line of interpretation includes Rush, *Still Interpreting Vatican II*, and John O'Malley, *What Happened at Vatican II?* For a criticism of that reading of Vatican II history, see Agostino Marchetto, *The Second Vatican Ecumenical Council*; Lamb and Levering, *Vatican II*; and Levering, *An Introduction to Vatican II as an Ongoing Theological Event*. For a response to critical readings of the Alberigo project, see Schultenover, *Vatican II*, especially the essays by Joseph A. Komonchak and John W. O'Malley, S.J. For a helpful guide through the literature on the reception of Vatican II, see Kaplan, "Vatican II as a Constitutional Text of Faith."

27. See Winter, "Jesus and Muhammad"; Madigan, "Mary and Muhammad"; and Ward, "Muhammad from a Christian Perspective."

28. In his 2005 Christmas address to the Roman Curia, Pope Benedict XVI called for a "hermeneutic of reform" in the interpretation of Vatican II instead of the "hermeneutic of discontinuity and rupture," which risks a split between the preconciliar and the postconciliar Church. This address was reprinted as the introduction to a collection of essays meant to follow the pope's lead on this issue. See Benedict XVI, "A Proper Hermeneutic for the Second Vatican Council," ix–x.

29. Benedict XVI, "A Proper Hermeneutic," xiii.

30. Like many of the other theological breakthroughs at Vatican II, scholarly work around this question had already begun before the Council. See especially the work of Louis Massignon. For an insightful overview of Massignon's work, see Krokus, *The Theology of Louis Massignon*, esp. 141–55. For Massignon's influence on Vatican II's pronouncements on Islam, see Krokus, "Louis Massignon's Influence on the Teaching of Vatican II on Muslims and Islam,"and Krokus, "Louis Massignon." For an alternative account of Massignon's influence on the Council, see D'Costa, *Vatican II*, 165–67, 180, and 186–87. Two of Massignon's students were influential in the drafting of the Council's language on this issue: Georges Anawati (1905–94) and Robert Caspar (1923–2007). It is worth noting that Massignon conceived of Muhammad as a "negative prophet," a term he did not make clear, such that several later thinkers have plausibly read into this term varying meanings (see Krokus, *The Theology of Louis Massignon*, 145–46).

31. Heft and O'Malley, "Introduction," xiii.

32. The members of the Doctrinal Commission noted that *DV* can be considered first among the constitutions of the Council. In reflecting on the final clause of no. 1, "so that by hearing the message of salvation the whole world may believe, by believing it may hope, and by hoping it may love," members of the commission said that this claim serves to introduce not just *DV* but the whole body of conciliar documents. See Vatican Council II, *Acta synodalia sacrosancti concilii oecumenici Vaticini II*, vol. 4, periodus 4, part 1, 341. Cf. Wicks, "Vatican II on Revelation," 641–48.

33. Vatican Council II, *Dei Verbum*, 8, 975. Hereafter, *DV*. All translations are from Tanner unless otherwise noted.

34. Vatican Council II, *Nostra Aetate*, 3, 969. Hereafter, *NA*.

35. Vatican Council II, *Lumen Gentium*, 16. Hereafter, *LG*.

36. While documents issued by the Congregation for the Doctrine of the Faith (CDF) do not have the authority to close avenues opened up by decrees of ecumenical councils, I accept relevant documents from both sources as authoritative. With respect to *Dominus Iesus* (*DI*), this book is, in the words of Francis Sullivan, a "response that respects the authority that the Pope has given

it by delegation and by confirmation." See Francis A. Sullivan, "Introduction and Ecclesiological Issues," 47.

37. Vatican II Council, *DV*, 11n5.

38. Montag, "Revelation," 46.

39. Aquinas, *Summa theologiae*, trans. Fathers of the English Dominican Province, *ST* II. II 174.4 *s.c.* and *co.*

40. *ST* II. II 174.6 *ad.* 3.

41. *ST* II. II 174.6 *ad.* 3.

42. Rahner, *Visions and Prophecies*, 21.

43. For a recent outstanding and helpful bibliography of modern studies of "prophecy" in English, see Hvidt, *Christian Prophecy*.

44. See Levering, *Participatory Biblical Exegesis*; *Scripture and Metaphysics*; *Christ's Fulfillment of Torah and Temple*; Dauphinais, *Aquinas the Augustinian*; Mattison, *Introducing Moral Theology*; Tapie, *Aquinas on Israel and the Church*; and Hütter and Levering, *Ressourcement Thomism*.

45. Troll, *Dialogue and Difference*, 117.

46. Ibid., 118–19.

47. Related questions about quranic interpretation will be mentioned but not resolved, as these fall outside the contours of the main argument of this book. These include how the Qur'an would challenge Christian beliefs and practices, how to approach quranic passages that directly contradict Christian revelation, and whether what is true in the Qur'an is true because Muhammad learned it from his encounters with Jews and Christians.

48. My own approach to this question in large part grows out of my participation in the practice of scriptural reasoning, in which Jews, Christians, and Muslims together read passages from Sacred Scripture that are gathered under a selected theme. For more information on the practice of scriptural reasoning and a list of resources, visit http://www.scripturalreasoning.org/. See also Ford and Pecknold, *The Promise of Scriptural Reasoning*.

49. See Moreland, "The Qur'an and the Doctrine of Private Revelation."

CHAPTER TWO. The State of the Question

1. For major scholarship conducted on Vatican II, see, for example, Alberigo and Komonchak, *History of Vatican II*; Alberigo et al., *The Reception of Vatican II*; Clifford, *Decoding Vatican II*; Wenger, *Vatican II*; Miller, *Vatican II*; O'Malley, *What Happened at Vatican II?*; Henri Fesquet, *The Drama of Vatican II*; and Scatena, *Vatican II*. For an alternative reading of the events of

Vatican II, see, for example, Matthew Lamb and Levering, *Vatican II*; Agostino Marchetto, *The Second Vatican Ecumenical Council*, trans. Whitehead; and Levering, *An Introduction to Vatican II as an Ongoing Theological Event.*

2. O'Malley, "Introduction," in Heft, *After Vatican II*, xiii.

3. Rush, "Toward a Comprehensive Interpretation of the Council and Its Documents."

4. Martin, "Revelation and Its Transmission," in Lamb and Levering, *Vatican II*, 55.

5. Vatican Council II, *Acta synodalia sacrosancti concilii oecumenici Vaticani II*, vol. 4, part 1, 341, quoted in Theobald, "The Theological Option of Vatican II," 91.

6. Ibid.

7. *DV* 1.

8. On the redaction history of the schema *De fontibus*, see Schelkens, *Catholic Theology of Revelation on the Eve of Vatican II.*

9. *DV* 1.

10. Farkasfalvy, "Inspiration and Interpretation," in Lamb and Levering, *Vatican II.*

11. Ibid., 79.

12. Cf. Romans 1:20.

13. *DV* 2.

14. Farkasfalvy, "Inspiration and Interpretation," 79.

15. *LG* 48 and 50, 5–67.

16. *DV* 9.

17. Vanhoye, "The Reception in the Church of the Dogmatic Constitution '*Dei Verbum*,'" in Granados, Granados, and Sanchez-Navarro, *Opening Up the Scriptures*, 109.

18. Vanhoye adds: "The rest of the phrase accentuates this effect of surprise, as the verb '*consignare*' is placed there in the present tense and not in the past, as one may have expected. The Special Commission had actually placed the past participle '*consignata*,' which seemed more logical, as the putting into writing of the divine message is a fact in the past; however, the use of '*consignata*' was criticized because, according to Alberto Franzini, 'this way of saying it could suggest an identification of the Word of God with its written form.' . . . In the end, the conciliar definition leads to a reversal of the relationships between the written text and the oral message. The word 'locutio' normally designates an oral message; it is applied by the Council to a written text, the text of the Bible." Vanhoye, "The Reception in the Church of the Dogmatic Constitution '*Dei Verbum*,'" in *Opening Up the Scriptures*, 106. Author is quoting Roger Schutz and Fr. Max Thurian. *La parole vivante au Concile.* (Taize, France: Presses de Taize, 1966), 120.

19. Vanhoye, "The Reception in the Church of the Dogmatic Constitution '*Dei Verbum*,'" in *Opening Up the Scriptures*, 106.

20. Barnes, "Opening Up a Dialogue," 18.

21. Benedict XVI, *Verbum Domini*, 17.

22. *DV* 4, 972.

23. Latourelle, *Theology of Revelation*, 469.

24. *DV* 13, 977.

25. Farkasfalvy, *Inspiration and Interpretation*, 188.

26. *DV* 5, 973.

27. Boeve, "Revelation, Scripture and Tradition."

28. *DV* 8, 974.

29. *DV* 25, 980.

30. Vanhoye, "The Reception in the Church of the Dogmatic Constitution '*Dei Verbum*,'" in *Opening Up the Scriptures*, 118. For an account of the "inspired reader," see U. H. J. Körtner, *Der Inspüerte Leser*, 1994).

31. Wright, "How Can the Bible Be Authoritative?," 21 and 22–23.

32. See "News Summary," *New York Times*, December 8, 1985, available at https://www.nytimes.com/1985/12/08/news/news-summary-sunday-december-8-1985.html.

33. *LG* 16.

34. Ibid.: *qui fidem Abrahae se tenere profitentes, nobiscum Deum adorant unicum, misericordem, homines die novissimo iudicaturum.*

35. See D'Costa, *Vatican II*, 166–180.

36. Ibid., 202.

37. Caspar, "Le Concile et l'Islam," 118. For a table presenting the Council teachings on Islam through Church history, see D'Costa, *Vatican II*, 169–70. See also Farrugia, *The Church and the Muslims*, 42–44.

38. I disagree with Mikka Ruokanen, who argues that "what is apparent to human reason has become an institutionalized religion in Islam" in his *The Catholic Doctrine of Non–Christian Religions according to the Second Vatican Council*, 78. Roukanen implies that *only* what is apparent to human reason emerges in Islam. In my reading of the conciliar texts, the overlapping web of beliefs about Mary, Jesus, eschatology, and so on, added to the fact that we "adore" the one God together, imply that Muslims do not come to know God just through natural reason.

39. Daniel Madigan, "Mutual Theological Hospitality," in El-Ansary and Linnan, *Muslim and Christian Understanding*, 58.

40. For an incisive critique of *Dominus Iesus* on this point, see Clooney, "Implications for the Practice of Inter-religious Learning," 157–68, esp. 159.

41. Madigan, "Saving *Dominus Iesus*," in *Learned Ignorance*, ed. Heft, Firestone, and Safi, 270.

42. *LG*, 17.

43. *LG*, 17. The version of *LG* published at the Vatican website inaccurately translates the Latin word "*propriis*" to "latent." A better translation of "*propriis*" in this instance is "particular," which more accurately expresses how truths may be readily evident in other religious traditions rather than hidden and inaccessible. For the translation provided by the Vatican, see Pope Paul VI, "*Lumen Gentium*," 17

44. Sullivan, "Vatican II on the Salvation of the Adherents of Other Religions," 76.

45. *NA* received 88 negative votes, 2,221 positive, and 3 invalid. On the struggles of its passage, see John W. O'Malley, *What Happened at Vatican II*, esp. 218–26, 277, and 308. While *NA* represents the climax of the Council's openness to non-Catholic religions, this orientation is found throughout the conciliar documents. Jacques Dupuis, S.J., highlights the pertinent texts in his "Interreligious Dialogue in the Church's Evangelizing Mission," 3:237–63, esp. 241–43. See also Jacques Dupuis, *Jesus Christ and His Spirit*, chap. 9, esp. 153–55, and chap. 11, esp. 196–202. John Oesterreicher provides a detailed account of the text's redaction process in *Commentary on the Documents of Vatican II*, vol. 3, 1–136. See also Alberigo and Komonchak's *History of Vatican II*, esp. G. Miccoli, "Two Sensitive Issues: Religious Freedom and the Jews," vol. 4, chap. 2, and Mauro Velati, "Completing the Conciliar Agenda," vol. 5, chap. 3. For a non-Catholic commentary on the development of the text, see Mikka Ruokanen, *The Catholic Doctrine of Non-Christian Religions according to the Second Vatican Council*.

46. *NA* 2.

47. Ibid.

48. Ibid.

49. Ibid.

50. Ibid., 3. I chose the unofficial translation from the Vatican website here since it follows the Latin more closely than the Tanner translation. See Pope Paul VI, *Nostra Aetate*: Declaration on the Revelation of the Church to Non-Christian Religions, October 28, 1965, available at www.vatican.va/. The original Latin is as follows: "Muslimos respicit qui unicum Deum adorant, viventem et subsistentem, misericordem et omnipotentem, Creatorem caeli et terrae (5), homines allocutum, cuius occultis etiam decretis toto animo se submittere student, sicut Deo se submisit Abraham ad quem fides islamica libenter sese refert. Iesum, quem quidem ut Deum non agnoscunt, ut prophetam tamen venerantur, matremque eius virginalem honorant Mariam et aliquando eam devote etiam invocant. Diem insuper iudicii expectant cum Deus omnes homines resuscitatos remunerabit. Exinde vitam moralem aestimant et Deum maxime in

oratione, eleemosynis et ieiunio colunt." And this is the Tanner translation: "They worship the one God living and subsistent, merciful and almighty, creator of heaven and earth, who has spoken to humanity and to whose decrees, even the hidden ones, they seek to submit themselves whole-heartedly, just as Abraham, to whom the Islamic faith readily relates itself, submitted to God. They venerate Jesus as a prophet, even though they do not acknowledge him as God, and they honour his virgin mother Mary and even sometimes devoutly call upon her. Furthermore they await the day of judgment when God will requite all people brought back to life. Hence they have regard for the moral life and worship God especially in prayer, almsgiving and fasting." Tanner, *Decrees of the Ecumenical Councils*, 969.

51. An earlier draft included "personal" as one of the shared characteristics of God, but it was deleted as its Arabic translation was misleading. See Gavin D'Costa's illuminating discussion in *Vatican II*, 202–3.

52. Caspar, "La religion musulamanne," *Unum Sanctum* 61 (Paris, 1966), 217.

53. D'Costa, *Vatican II*, 202–3.

54. Caspar, "La religion musulamanne," 220.

55. Ibid., 218.

56. Caspar notes, "Les opinions actuelles des théoriciens chrétiens sons assez divergentes. Disons seulement que la foi catholique exclut les révélations constitutives du dépôt de la foi depuis la mort du dernier apôtre (Dz, 783; 2021), mais n'exclut pas des 'révélations' au sens large, que sont des motions de l'Esprit, des 'charismes,' visant au progrès de la foi et de la charité, dans l'Eglise et même en dehors de ses limites visibles. Le cas de Mohammed et de la 'révélation' coranique es un des plus ambigus." Caspar, "La religion musulmanne," 219.

57. D'Costa, *Vatican II*, 204–5. In addition, *NA* 3 refers to *"fides islamica."* Some argue that Islam is affirmed in this paragraph by the use of the word "submission" (*submittere*). Others argue that Flannery's and Tanner's translations have obscured the explicit reference to Islam. See D'Costa, *Vatican II*, 167nn28–29, drawing upon Andrew Unsworth's unpublished dissertation. See Unsworth, "A Historical and Textual-Critical Analysis of the Magisterial Documents of the Catholic Church on Islam." See Vatican Council II, *The Conciliar and Postconciliar Documents*, trans. Austin Flannery (Northpoint, NY: 1996).

58. Curiously, *NA* does not mention the Qur'an, Muhammad, or Islam, but rather restricts itself to "Muslims." The Muslim beliefs that *NA* highlights and applauds are, however, delivered by the Prophet Muhammad and documented in the Qur'an. See Madigan, "Jesus and Muhammad," 90–99, and Anna Bonta Moreland, "An Analogical Reading of Christian Prophecy," 62–75.

59. Laurentin, *The Apparitions of the Blessed Virgin Mother Today*, 19.

60. Michael Barnes, "Opening Up a Dialogue," 28.

61. In a provocative essay, "Learning From (and Not Just About) Our Religious Neighbors: Comparative Theology and the Future of *Nostra Aetate*," John Thatamanil suggests a thoughtful rewriting of *NA* in which the verb "receive" is added to what the Church asks of her sons and daughters in the second paragraph of *NA*. In this paragraph, the Council asks Christians to "recognize, preserve and promote the good things, spiritual and moral, as well as the socio-cultural values found among these" (*NA* 2). Thatamanil suggests that if "receive" were added to this list of verbs, *NA* would be saved from a religious "self-sufficiency" that inhibits it from being genuinely dialogical. See Thatamanil in Cohen, Knitter, and Rosenhagen, eds., *The Future of Interreligious Dialogue: A Multireligious Conversation on* Nostra Aetate (Maryknoll, NY: Orbis, 2017), 166–72 at 167.

62. Pope Benedict XVI, "*Verbum Domini.*" Post-Synodal Apostolic Exhortation, no. 14, 58, quoting *DV* 8. I am grateful to Michael Barnes, S.J., for pointing me toward this Apostolic Exhortation in his "Opening Up a Dialogue," 29.

63. Benedict XVI, foreword to Hvidt, *Christian Prophecy*, viii.

64. For a lucid and brief overview of Christian-Muslim dialogue in the twenty years following the Council, see Anawati, "An Assessment of the Christian-Islamic Dialogue," 51–68. For an overview of the work of the Groupe de Recherches Islamo-Chrétien (GRIC), which was formed in 1977 by a small number of Christian and Muslim colleagues who worked together on common research projects framed by Muslim-Christian dialogue, see *Islamochristiana* 4, 175–86; Muslim-Christian Research Group, *The Challenge of the Scriptures*, trans. Brown; Pontificio Istituto di Studi Arabi e d'Islamistica, "General Guidelines for True Dialogue," 9–14.

65. Fitzgerald, "'Dialogue and Proclamation,'" 181–93, at 183. See also Siddiqui, *Christian-Muslim Dialogue in the Twentieth Century*, 35.

66. Dhavamony, "Evangelization and Dialogue in Vatican II and in the 1974 Synod," 3:264–81, at 273–74. For Gerald O'Collins, the conciliar documents affirm that "God's self-communication includes a *revelatory* dimension . . . and a *salvific* dimension" (*The Second Vatican Council on Other Religions*, 81).

67. Dupuis, "Interreligious Dialogue in the Church's Evangelizing Mission," 3:256.

68. PCID, *Guidelines for Dialogue between Christians and Muslims*, 57.

69. Ibid., 58. Emphasis in original.

70. It should be noted that Cardinal Joseph Ratzinger was then the head of the CDF. As such, he made observations during the process of drafting the document and approved its publication. See Dupuis, "A Theological Commentary," 119–60, at 122.

71. Vatican Council II, *Ad gentes* 11.

72. Pontifical Council for Interreligious Dialogue, *Interreligious Dialogue* no. 16, 613–14.

73. Dupuis notes a tension in this document between (1) the recognition of interreligious dialogue as a true form of the Church's mission and (2) the centrality and necessity of proclamation, always required in evangelization: "The question must be asked how interreligious dialogue can *by itself*, prior to, and eventually in the absence of proclamation, be a genuine form of evangelization, if proclamation needs to be present *always*, as its *simultaneous foundation* without which 'there is no true evangelization.'" Dupuis, "A Theological Commentary," 146 (Emphasis in original).

74. Benedict XVI, "Meeting with Representatives of Some Muslim Communities."

75. On the one hand, *DI* 2, referring to *NA* 2, states: "The Catholic Church rejects nothing of what is *true* and *holy* in these religions" (emphasis added). On the other hand: "On the basis of such presuppositions, which may evince different nuances, certain theological proposals are developed—at times presented as assertions, and at times as hypotheses—in which Christian revelation and the mystery of Jesus Christ and the Church lose their character of absolute truth and salvific universality, or at least shadows of doubt and uncertainty are cast upon them" (*DI* 4).

76. Congregation for the Doctrine of the Faith, *Dominus Iesus*, 3.

77. Pope John Paul II, *DI* 7, in Denzinger, *Compendium of Creeds, Definitions, and Declarations on Matters of Faith and Morals*, 43 and 1138.

78. Clooney, "Implications for the Practice of Inter-religious Learning," 157–68, at 158–59.

CHAPTER THREE. Thomas Aquinas on Prophecy

1. Thomas's treatment of prophecy arises in three principal texts: the *DVer* (q. 12), the *ScG*, and *ST* (II-II, 171–74), along with his biblical commentaries on Isaiah, the Gospel of John, 1 Corinthians, and Hebrews.

2. Elders, "Les rapports entre la doctrine de la prophétie de saint Thomas," 449–56; Torrell, *Thomas d'Aquin*, 15–19; and Zarb "Le fonti agostiniane," *Angelicum* 15 (1938): 169–200.

3. Magno, *Quaestio de prophetia*; Altmann, "Maimonides and Thomas Aquinas," *Association for Jewish Studies Review* 3 (1978): 1–19; Pérez, "Acerca de la verdad contenida en la Sagrada Escritura," 393–424; Casciaro, *El diálogo de Santo Tomás con Musulmanes y Judíos*; Casciaro, "Santo Tomás ante sus fuentes," 11–65; and Nader, "L'Influence de la pensée musulmane sur la

philosophie de Saint Thomas d'Aquin," 61–68. Aquinas paid more attention than did his contemporaries to the psychology of inspiration and prophecy. He drew on Aristotle's psychology and devoted "extraordinary attention to the data of Scripture concerning prophetic experience," offering four or five times more biblical citations than Albert the Great or Hugh of Saint Cher; "Aquinas integrates fully the prophetic charism into the history of revelation, something which is not at all evident in reading theological expositions in the thirteenth century." Torrell, "Les Charismes au service de la révélation."

4. See MacIntyre, *Whose Justice? Which Rationality?*, 167.

5. Burtchaell, *Catholic Theories of Biblical Inspiration since 1810*; Zerafa, "The Limits of Biblical Inerrancy," 92–119; Benoit and Synave, *Saint Thomas d'Aquin*; Benoit, "Révélation et inspiration," 321–70; Brian McCarthy, "El modo del conocimiento profético," 425–84; and Andrés Ibáñez Arana, "Las Cuestiones 'De Prophetia' en Santo Tomás y la Inspiración Bíblica," 256–312. For a helpful overview of this literature, see Rogers, "Thomas Aquinas and Prophecy," 3–7.

6. *ScG* I.6: *quin potius vera quae docuit multis fabulis et falsissimis doctrinis immiscuit.*

7. Ibid.: *quod eius dictis fidem adhibentes leviter credunt.*

8. See *ST* II.II 12.1.1, *Super Psalmo* 2.6, and 1 Cor. 15.I.1.

9. For a complex account of European medieval attitudes toward Muhammad, see Tolan, *Mahomet l'Européen*, especially chaps 1–4.

10. *ST* II.II 174.4 *s.c.* and *co.*

11. *ST* II.II 174.6 *ad.* 3.

12. Ibid.

13. For an insightful treatment of the structural parallels between prophecy and *sacra doctrina* in Thomas, see Rogers, "Thomas Aquinas and Prophecy," esp. 12–40.

14. I agree with Frederick Bauerschmidt when he advocates for understanding the term for salvation in Latin, "*salus*," to cover a broader meaning than just the eternal salvation of human beings. The Latin root of *salus* means "health" or "well-being." While this initial article of the *ST* highlights *salus* as the final end of all human living, throughout the corpus one sees *salus* used in the broader sense of human flourishing. This emerges in the treatment of prophecy such that prophetic revelation primarily concerns supernatural knowledge, but it can also extend to certain things known through natural reason. Cf. Frederick Bauerschmidt, *Holy Teaching*, 32n7. Prophets receive everything necessary to teach the people about the gift of faith.

15. *ST* I.1.8 *ad.* 2.

16. *ST* I.1.2.

17. In church history, prophecy was linked with predicting future events. But Bernard McGinn finds that in early medieval Christianity the "broadest and most significant function of prophecy . . . was its identification with the spiritual interpretation of the Bible and preaching." McGinn, "Prophetic Power in Early Medieval Christianity," *Cristianesimo nella storia* 17 (1996): 251–69, at 269. Thomas distinguishes himself from his contemporaries, however, in not restricting the proper sense of prophecy to a foretelling of future events. See Hugh of Saint-Cher, *De prophetia*, Q.481, a.1, *ad*. 9, as cited in Torrell, *Théorie de la prophétie et philosophie de la connaissance aux environs de 1230*, 16 11.1–11.12.

18. *ST* II. II 171.6: *prophetia est quaedam cognitio intellectui prophetae impressa ex revelatio divina per modum cuiusdam doctrinae.*

19. *ST* II. II 171.1.

20. *ST* II. II 171.6.

21. *Super Evangelium S. Ioannis lectura*, 1.18, 221, cited by Emery in *The Trinitarian Theology of St. Thomas Aquinas*, 202. I am grateful to Paul Martin Rogers, whose dissertation, "Thomas Aquinas and Prophecy," pointed me toward this text.

22. *ScG* III.154.4.

23. The classification of prophecy as a gratuitous grace becomes more central in the *Prima Secundae* of the *ST* than in the *DVer*, as it is placed within the treatise of gratuitous graces. In the prior work Thomas distinguishes prophecy from sanctifying grace in response to an objection and mentions *gratia gratis datae* in two places, but, both structurally and substantively, the fact that prophecy is gratuitous grace is not yet accentuated. For an insightful commentary on grace in Aquinas, see Wawrykow, *God's Grace and Human Action*, and for a helpful summary of the role of the Holy Spirit in the gifts of grace see Colberg, "Aquinas and the Grace of Auxilium," 187–210.

24. *ST* I. II 111.1, 4. For Thomas's commentary on 1 Cor. 12:8–10, see Aquinas, *Super I Epistolam B. Pauli ad Corinthios lectura*, 987–1046.

25. *ST* II. II 171.1.

26. *ScG* III 154.8.

27. Rogers, "Thomas Aquinas and Prophecy," 10.

28. *ST* I. II 111.4 *ad*. 4.

29. *ST* II. II 172.1 *ad*. 4.

30. *ST* II. II 81.8.

31. *DVer* 12.2. While prophecy is wide-ranging for Thomas, it is more proper to knowledge than to action (cf. *ST* I. II 174.3).

32. *DVer* 12.3.

33. *DVer* 12.1, in 1 Cor., chap.12, lect.1, *ST* II. II 171.1.

34. "For the one who is now called a prophet was formerly called a seer" (1 Sam. 9:9).

35. I am grateful to Brian McCarthy for tracing the etymological roots with which Thomas was working in his treatment of prophecy (see his "El modo del conocimiento profético," 445n51).

36. *ST* II.II 174.1.

37. Rogers, "Thomas Aquinas and Prophecy," 170.

38. *Cf.* Moreland, *Known by Nature*, 128.

39. *ST* II.II 173.1.

40. Ibid.

41. *ST* II.II 171.3; *DVer* 12.2.

42. *ST* II.II 171.4.

43. *DVer* 12.12.

44. *ST* II.II 171.4 *ad. 2: Prophetia est sicut quiddam imperfectum in genere divinae revelationis, unde dicitur I ad Cor. XIII, quod prophetiae evacuabuntur, et quod ex parte prophetamus, id est imperfecte. Perfectio autem divinae revelationis erit in patria, unde subditur, cum venerit quod perfectum est, evacuabitur quod ex parte est. Unde non oportet quod propheticae revelatio nihil de sit, sed quod nihil de siteorum ad quae prophetia ordinatur.*

45. Aquinas, *Commentary on the First Epistle to the Corinthians*, par. 788, available at: http://dhspriory.org/.

46. *ScG* III 154, par. 25.

47. *ST* II.II 171.1 *ad. 4: Sic igitur ad prophetiam requiritur inspiratio quantum ad mentis elevationem, secundum illud Iob XXXII, inspiratio omni potentis dat intelligentiam, revelatio autem, quantum ad ipsam perceptionem divinorum, in quo perficitur prophetia.*

48. *ST* II.II 171.2.

49. Ibid. In the reply to the eighth difficulty of *DVer* 12.1, for example, we read, "*Quod ratio illa procederet si lumen quo perfunditur mens prophetae, esset habitus; non autem si ponimus habilitatem ad percipiendum lumen praedicutm esse habitum, vel quasi habitum; cum ex eodem possit esse aliquis habilis ut illuminetur de quocumque.*"

50. One can see Thomas here at pains to distinguish proper prophetic revelations from visions that arise from mental illness, where a person is "thrown off her mental balance [*mente perturbata*], like persons who are possessed" (*ST* II.II 173.3 *ad.* 4).

51. Rogers, "Thomas Aquinas and Prophecy," 147.

52. *ST* II.II 173.3.

53. *DVer* 12.13.

54. *ST* II.II 173.2.

55. *DVer* 12.7.

56. Casciaro, "Santo Tomás ante sus fuentes," 57–61.

57. McCarthy, "El modo del conocimiento profético," 436n24.

58. I follow Torrell's analysis of dates. See Torrell, *Saint Thomas Aquinas*, 12–28 and 146.

59. Aquinas, *In Isaiam* (hereafter, *In Is.*), *cap.* 1.1, in *Sancti Thomae de Aquino opera omnia.*

60. McCarthy notes that when Thomas wrote the Isaiah commentary he had already learned a considerable amount of Aristotelian philosophy at the Dominicans' *studium generale* in Cologne, and, as a result, he already knew how to distinguish between the two aspects of the cognoscitive act. But he also carried with him the weight of the Christian tradition, whose epistemology was different. While Thomas let the tradition guide his Isaiah commentary, by the time he wrote Q. 12 of the *DVer*, he clearly distinguished between the double act of the intellect (*DVer* 12.3 *ad.* 1, 12.7). All later works follow the *DVer* in this respect. See McCarthy, "El modo del conocimiento profético," 444–45, n48.

61. Ibid., 447.

62. Ibid., 448.

63. *ST* II. II 174.6.

64. Ibid.

65. Ibid.

66. *ST* II. II 174.6 *ad.* 3. Cf. *De Civ. Dei* v, 26.

67. *ST* II. II 172.2 *ad.* 1.

68. *DVer* 12.8.

69. *ST* II. II 174.6 *ad.* 3: *Et singulis temporibus non defuerunt aliqui prophetiae spiritum habentes, non quidem ad novam doctrinam fidei depromendam, sed ad humanorum actuum directionem.*

70. In the *DVer* (12.4 *ad.* 6), Thomas insists that even some who lack charity might be better disposed than good people. They might, for example, be more fit to perceive spiritual things because they are free from carnal affections and worldly cares, and they might possess a certain knack for understanding. Thomas does not go into such explicit detail in the *ST* (II. II 172.3).

71. *ST* II. II 172.4.

72. *DVer* 12.5 *ad.* 2: *Quamvis prophetia sit spiritus sancti donum, non tamen cum dono prophetiae spiritus sanctus datur, sed solummodo cum dono caritatis.*

73. There is a parallel here between prophets who choose to misuse the prophecy and pagan philosophers who had knowledge of God but refused to worship Him. See my *Known by Nature*, 136.

74. *ST* II. II 172.5: *Et ideo prophetia proprie et simpliciter dicta fit solum per revelationem divinam. Sed et ipsa revelatio facta per Daemones, potest secundum quid dici prophetia.*

75. *ST* II. II 172.6 *ad.* 1: *Quia Deus utitur etiam malis ad utilitatem bonorum.*

76. Ibid.: *Unde et per prophetas Daemonum aliqua vera praenuntiat, tum ut credibilior fiat veritas, quae etiam ex adversariis testimonium habet; tum etiam quia, dum homines talibus credunt, per eorum dicta magis ad veritatem inducuntur.*

77. *ScG* III 154.21.

78. *ST* II. II 174.4 *s.c., co.*

79. *ST* II. II 171.5.

80. *ST* II. II 174.3 *ad.* 2

81. *DVer* 12.4.

CHAPTER FOUR.   Scriptural Prophets and Muhammad

1. John 11:49–53.

2. Aquinas, *In Io.* 11.7.

3. John 12:37 and 43, which are cited in *In Io.* 11.7.

4. Thomas here sides with Chrysostom's interpretation over Augustine's. Augustine thought that if everyone believed in Christ, there would be no one left to defend the temple against the Romans because they would have abandoned the temple and the laws of their ancestors and instead would have replaced them with Christ's teaching against these laws. See Augustine, *Tract. in Io.,* n195.

5. The Deuteronomic text that Thomas cites in his commentary differs from the NRSV (*The Holy Bible: The New Revised Standard Version, Catholic Edition*). I have cited the biblical text as it appears in the English translation of Thomas's commentary (*Si fuerit in medio tui propheta, aut qui somnium vidisse se dicat, et voluerit te a domino retrahere, propheta ille, ut fictor somniorum, interficiatur.*). The NRSV has: "If prophets or those who divine by dreams appear among you and promise you omens or portents, and the omens or the portents declared by them take place, and they say, 'Let us follow other gods' (whom you have not known) 'and let us serve them,' you must not heed the words of those prophets or those who divine by dreams; for the Lord your God is testing you, to know whether you indeed love the Lord your God with all your heart and soul."

6. *In Io.* 11, *Lectio* 7.

7. Ibid.

8. A businesswoman, for example, could pay her employees a just wage and yet act fundamentally unjustly toward her spouse, her children, her neighbors, etc. One would not call her "just" even if her employees could not complain about their wages.

9. *In Io.* 11, *Lectio 7*.

10. These were Gideon, Barak, Samson, Jephthah, David, and Samuel.

11. Aquinas, *Super Heb.*, *cap.* 11.1.7. I modified this translation to make it closer to the Latin: *Quando autem non cognoscit, non est vere propheta, sed participative tantum. Et sic dicit Ioannes Caipham prophetasse, quia habuit aliquid prophetiae. Iste autem motus spiritus sancti dicitur instinctus secundum Augustinum.*

12. *Super I Cor.*, *cap.* 12.1.1.

13. *ST* II. II 173.4 *sc.*

14. *ST* II. II 173.4.

15. *Gen. ad lit.* xi and 29 as cited in *ST* II. II 165.2.

16. Ibid. *ad.* 4: *sicut asina in qua sedebat Balaam, locuta est homini, nisi quod illud fuit opus diabolicum, hoc angelicum.*

17. *Quaestiones Disputatae De Potentia Dei* 6.5 *ad.* 3. English translation: *On the Power of God*, trans. English Dominican Fathers (Westminster, MD: Newman, 1932), hereafter, *DePot.*

18. Aquinas, *Super I Epistolam B. Pauli ad Corinthios*, ch. 12.1.

19. *Quaestiones Disputatae De Veritate* 12.3 *ad.* 1. English translation: *On Truth*, trans. Robert W. Mulligan, S.J. (Chicago: Henry Regnery, 1952), hereafter, *De Ver.*

20. *ST* 172.6 *sc.*

21. *ST* 172.6 *ad.* 1. Thomas also writes, "Wherefore also the Sibyls [Sibyllae] foretold many true things about Christ."

22. *ST* II. II 174.1 *arg.* 3.

23. Aquinas, *Commentary on the Letter of Saint Paul to the Hebrews* I.1.

24. *Commentary on the First Epistle to the Corinthians* 14.1: *Et sic Salomon et David possunt dici prophetae, inquantum habuerunt lumen intellectuale, ad clare et subtiliter intuendum.*

25. *DVer* 12.12: *Quandoque igitur in prophetia non est aliqua supernaturalis acceptio, sed iudicium tantum supernaturale; et sic solus intellectus illustratur sine aliqua imaginaria visione. Et talis forte fuit inspiratio Salomonis, inquantum de moribus hominum et naturis rerum, quae naturaliter accipimus, divino instinctu ceteris certius iudicavit.*

26. *ST* II. II 173.2.

27. *ST* II. II 174.2.

28. 2 Kgs. 5:26.

29. *ST* III 7.8.

30. For a lucid argument of how the work of Christ entails beatific know-ing, see Wilkins, "Love and Knowledge of God in the Human Life of Christ."

31. *ST* III 7.8 *ad.* 2.

32. *ST* III 11.1.

33. *ST* II. II 174.6.3.

34. Hvidt, *Christian Prophecy*, 78.

35. Pontifical Council for Interreligious Dialogue, *Dialogue and Procla-mation*, 37. Fruitful analogical reasoning is already conducted from both Christian and Muslim quarters. From the Muslim perspective, Joseph Lum-bard explores how an analogical approach to the Word of God in Jesus and the Qur'an helps to deepen both traditions' understanding of themselves and each other. See Lumbard, "What of the Word Is in Common?," 106. A recognition of the analogical reasoning in this essay would have addressed Maria Dakake's concerns in her response to this essay in the same volume. Dakake warns that to Muslim ears the "Word" of the Qur'an never connotes creation in the sense that things are created through the Qur'an, as it does when Christians speak of God creating through the Word. This is precisely the move that interfaith analo-gous reasoning recognizes. There is a genuine overlap, a resonance, between Jesus and the Qur'an as Word of God. But this is against a backdrop of crucial differences. Outlining these points of resonance and difference is the task of creative interfaith groups like the "A Common Word" initiative. The analogi-cal reasoning present in Dakake's essay, which explicates the Adamic and Christic nature in all of us, is a compelling instantiation of the kind of reason-ing I am suggesting here (Dakake, "Theological Parallels and Metaphysical Meeting Points," 135). From the Christian perspective, Pim Valkenberg reads al-Ghazālī and Said Nursi and notices analogies between those texts and Chris-tian theological and spiritual notions. See Valkenberg, *Sharing Lights on the Way to God*.

CHAPTER FIVE.   Is Muhammad a Prophet for Christians?

1. While the list of theologians whose works are discussed in this chapter is not exhaustive, it is representative of Christian attempts to address this ques-tion. Other notable instances include Claude Geffré's contribution to the Sec-ond Muslim-Christian meeting in Tunis in 1979. Geffré suggested that the reve-lation that came through Muhammad was *a word of God*, while Christ contains in himself *the Word of God*. In addition, the theologians who comprised the

GRIC (Groupe de Recherche Islamo-Chrétien) concluded that the Qur'an contains the word of God, which is "genuine but different" from the Word of God who is Jesus Christ. See GRIC, *The Challenge of the Scriptures*. For a brief overview of other attempts to further address this question by papal statements and local episcopates see Troll, *Muslims Ask, Christians Answer*, 38–39.

2. Watt, *Muhammad*, 17.

3. Ibid., 232.

4. Ibid., 234.

5. Ibid., 236.

6. Ibid., 237.

7. It is noteworthy that in a later (1991) work Watt claims that "it is widely held that Islam has been more successful than Christianity in bringing religious and oral values to bear on political life" (*Muslim-Christian Encounters*, 137).

8. Watt, *Muhammad*, 238.

9. Ibid., 239.

10. Ibid., 240.

11. Watt, *Muslim-Christian Encounters*, 133.

12. Ibid., 133–34.

13. Watt, *Islam and Christianity*, 60–61.

14. Ibid.

15. Ibid.

16. Watt, *Muslim-Christian Encounters*, 138–39.

17. Ibid., 29. In the same work, Watt curiously claims, "When one sees a poor Indian cripple boy begging with a serenely happy smile on his face, one is bound to acknowledge that a religion which achieves this for him is worthy of admiration" (139).

18. Watt, *Muslim-Christian Encounters*, 28.

19. Ibid.

20. Ibid., 142.

21. Ibid., 25.

22. Ibid., 27.

23. Ibid., 29.

24. Ibid., 148.

25. Watt, *Muhammad*, 17.

26. Watt, *Muslim-Christian Encounters*, 145.

27. Küng, "Towards an Ecumenical Theology of Religions," 129.

28. Ibid., 124.

29. Ibid., 125.

30. Ibid.

31. Ibid.
32. Ibid.
33. Ibid., 126.
34. Ibid.
35. Ibid., 127.
36. Ibid., 127–28.
37. Ibid., 129.
38. Ibid.
39. Küng, *Islam: Past, Present and Future*, 118.
40. Ibid., 118.
41. Ibid., 123.
42. Ibid., 124. For an account of the kinship between the three Abrahamic religions, see also Küng's "Radical Changes in History," 93–102.
43. Mahmut Aydin mistakenly concludes that Cragg changed his hermeneutic from *The Call of the Minaret* to *Muhammad and the Christian*. After citing a passage that Cragg summarizes as a position *not his own*, Aydin concludes that "Cragg seems to move away from assessing the phenomenon of Muhammad in the light of Christian teaching to an assessment in the light of the Qur'an's own teaching" ("Contemporary Christian Evaluations of the Prophet Muhammad," 38). While Cragg does admit that Islam has its own frame of reference for doctrinal issues, he does not go the way of incommensurability between religions. Instead he suggests, "It is one thing—a necessary one—to avoid 'Christianizing' what is properly and vigorously distinctive in Islam. It is another to conclude that, therefore, the disparate faiths are incommunicado. If there is a 'venture of Islam,' may there not duly be a venture *into* it and *with* it?" Cragg, *Muhammad and the Christian*, 12–13.
44. "So let the People of the Gospel judge by what God has sent down in it. Whoever does not judge by what God has sent down, those—they are wicked." *The Qur'ān*, trans. A. J. Droge, 69.
45. Cragg, *Muhammad and the Christian*, 122.
46. Cragg, *The Call of the Minaret*, 75.
47. In his *Muhammad and the Christian*, for example, Cragg urges Christians to "maintain our steady witness, for Islam's own sake, to religious dimensions which must always elude the power-equation" (140).
48. Cragg, *Muhammad and the Christian*, 47.
49. Ibid., 92.
50. Ibid., 98.
51. Ibid., 87.
52. Khan, "Metatheological Reflections," 190–91.
53. Cragg, *Muhammad and the Christian*, 7.

54. Ibid., 108.
55. Ibid., 152.
56. Ibid., 109.
57. Cragg, *The Weight in the Word*, 5.
58. Cragg, *Muhammad and the Christian*, 109.
59. Kerr, "The Prophet Muhammad," 114.
60. Ibid., 114–15.
61. Ibid., 115.
62. Kerr, "He Walked in the Path of the Prophets," 441.
63. Ibid.
64. Ibid.
65. Ibid.
66. Kerr, "Muhammad," 141.
67. Ibid., 142–43.
68. Ibid., 148.
69. Ibid., 155.
70. Kerr, "Muhammad," 155. Cf. Küng, *Christianity and the World Religions*, 129.
71. Ibid., 158, citing Khodr, "L'Arabité," 189.
72. Ibid., 159.
73. Ibid., 160.
74. Ibid., 161.
75. Ibid., 163.
76. Ibid., 165.
77. Ibid., 167.
78. Ibid.
79. Ibid., 168.
80. Ibid., 169.
81. Jomier, *The Great Themes of the Qur'an*, 17.
82. *ST* II-II.172.1. *ad* 4.
83. Troll, *Dialogue and Difference*, 117.
84. Ibid., 118–19.
85. Ibid., 119.
86. Ibid.
87. Ibid., 119–120.
88. Ibid., 120.
89. Ibid.
90. Ibid.
91. Ibid.
92. Ibid., 126.

93. Ibid., 128.
94. Troll, *Muslims Ask, Christians Answer*, 39.
95. Ibid., 40–41.
96. Ibid., 41.
97. Ibid.
98. Ibid., 41–42.
99. Ibid.
100. Ibid.
101. Ibid., 43.
102. Jomier, *How to Understand Islam*, 140–141.
103. Ibid., 143.
104. Ibid., 144.
105. Ibid., 146.
106. Ibid., citing Toynbee, *The World and the West*.
107. Ibid., 146–47.
108. Ibid.
109. Ibid.
110. Ibid., 148.
111. Ibid.

CHAPTER SIX.   Closing Argument

1. *New American Bible.*
2. An *apologion* itself is already tied to one's reasons for hope (see Benedict XVI's gloss on this text in *Spe Salvi*, para. 2).
3. For excellent work on Aquinas and analogy see Lyttkens, *The Analogy between God and the World*; Klubertanz, *St. Thomas Aquinas on Analogy*; Mc-Inerny, *The Logic of Analogy* and his more recent *Aquinas and Analogy*; and Montagnes, *La Doctrine de l'analogie de l'être d'après Saint Thomas d'Aquin.*
4. See, in particular, Burrell, *Aquinas: God and Action*; *Knowing the Unknowable God*; and *Freedom and Creation in Three Traditions.*
5. We must recognize that this is not a move that Thomas himself makes. Given his limited knowledge of Muslim belief and practice, he includes Muslims under the category of "unbelievers" in the beginning of the *ScG* (Book 1, chapter 2). Thomas Hibbs has persuasively argued that Aquinas did not write the *ScG* as a missionary manual to convert Muslims. See Hibbs, *Dialectic and Narrative in Aquinas*, 9–14.
6. *ST*, I, 13, 5: *Respondeo dicendum quod impossibile est aliquid praedicari de Deo et creaturis univoce. Quia omnis effectus non adaequans virtutem*

causaea gentis, recipit similitudinem a gentis non secundum eandem rationem, sed deficienter, ita ut quod divisim et multipliciter est in effectibus, in causa est simpliciter et eodemmodo; sicut sol secundum unam virtutem, multi formes et varias formas in istis inferioribus producit. . . . Sed necetiam pure aequivoce, ut aliquid ixerunt. Quia secundum hoc, ex creaturis nihil posset cognosci de Deo, nec demonstrari; sed semper incideret fallacia aequivocationis.

7. *ST,* I, 13, 6: *Unde, secundum hoc, dicendum est quod, quantum ad rem significatam per nomen, per prius dicuntur de Deo quam de creaturis, quia a Deo huiusmodi perfectiones in creaturas manant. Sed quantum ad impositionem nominis, per prius a nobis imponuntur creaturis, quas prius cognoscimus. Unde et modum significandi habent qui competit creaturis, ut supra dictum est.*

8. Burrell, "Analogy, Creation, and Theological Language," 35.

9. In this book I am pursuing the more modest proposal of speaking analogously in the Abrahamic traditions. There is no reason, in principle, not to apply this practice to other faith traditions. A creative example of this move can be found in Clooney, *Hindu God, Christian God,* and his *Divine Mary, Blessed Mother.*

10. See the collection of essays in *The Myth of Christian Uniqueness,* ed. Hick and Knitter, and *The Myth of Religious Superiority,* ed. Knitter.

11. See *Christian Uniqueness Reconsidered,* ed. D'Costa, and "Whose Objectivity? Which Neutrality?," ed. D'Costa, 79–95.

12. Burrell, "Faith, Culture, and Reason," 4.

13. Ibid., 5.

14. Ibid., 10.

15. Burrell, "Argument in Theology," 45–46.

16. Ibid., 46.

17. Williams, *On Christian Theology,* 94.

18. Burrell, "Argument in Theology," 47.

19. Christian Troll argues that Christians could never revere Muhammad as a prophet because, understood in the Islamic sense, Christians would have to obey him unconditionally. Instead, Troll invites Christians to "discern whatever is true, good and beautiful in the message of Islam and to respect the spiritual path followed by Muslims." Christians can even "acknowledge that Muhammad was a religious and political genius and should also be prepared to admit that through God's grace, countless believers have been inspired by the Qur'an and the life of the Prophet Muhammad to live their lives in a genuine relationship with God." See Troll, "Catholicism and Islam," in *The Catholic Church and the World Religions,* ed. D'Costa, 97. As an alternative to this approach, I am asking Christians here to mine the conciliar documents and the Christian understanding of prophecy in order to be open to the theoretical possibility that Muhammad was a prophet in a limited and relative manner.

20. *Catechism of the Catholic Church* no. 67.

21. Benedict XVI, "*Verbum Domini*," no.14.

22. Pope John Paul II, *Ut unum sint*, no. 80.

23. Rahner, *Visions and Prophecies*, 15.

24. Ibid., 16.

25. Heb. 1:1.

26. Jn. 1:29.

27. 1 Cor. 12:28. Among New Testament references on the role of prophets, we find Acts 2:18, 11:28, 19:6, 21:11; 1 Pt. 1:11; 2 Pt. 1:21.

28. Hvidt, *Christian Prophecy*, 60.

29. Küng, "The Charismatic Structure of the Church," 30–31.

30. *ST* 2-2, q. 171, a. 6.

31. Rahner maintained that a theology of private revelation would always occur within the framework of the charismatic element of the Church. See his "Revelation," 1471–1473.

32. *ST* 2-2, q. 174, a. 6, *ad*. 3.

33. Hvidt, *Christian Prophecy*, 78.

34. Bernard McGinn, "Prophetic Power in Early Medieval Christianity," 269.

35. Benedict XIV, *Benedicti papae XIV doctrina de servorum Dei beatificatione et beatorum canonizatione in synopsim redacta ab emm. de Azevedo*, 1.2, ch. 32n11, as cited in Staehlin, *Apariciones*, 40–41, translation mine. Benedict XIV wrote this magisterial study after twenty years of experience as Promoter of the Faith for the Causes of Beatification and Canonization (Staehlin, *Apariciones*, 40, n34).

36. Rahner, *Visions and Prophecies*, 18; Volken, *Visions, Revelations, and the Church*, 11–13; Dulles, *The Assurance of Things Hoped For*, 198; Suh, *Le rivelazioni private nella vita della Chiesa*, 32; Adnès, "Révélations Privées," 13:482–492. These theologians draw upon the language adopted by the Council of Trent. Denzinger, *The Sources of Catholic Dogma*, trans. Deferrari (hereafter, *DS*), 1540, 1566).

37. Hvidt, *Christian Prophecy*, 12.

38. Dulles, *The Assurance of Things Hoped For*, 198.

39. I do not mean to imply here that revelation is no longer about truth claims. Gerald O'Collins puts this shift nicely: "Even if the personal question (*Who* is revealed?) remains the primary one, the propositional content of revelation (the answer to the question '*What* is revealed?') has its proper place. The personal model emphasizes the *knowledge of* God (a knowledge by acquaintance) that the event of revelation embodies. But this implies that the believer enjoys a *knowledge about* God. The communication of truth *about* God be-

longs essentially to revelation, even if always at the service of the personal experience *of God* or encounter *with God*" (*Rethinking Fundamental Theology*, 67, emphasis in original).

40. Hvidt, *Christian Prophecy*, 31.

41. Rahner, "Death of Jesus and the Closure of Revelation," 140–141.

42. Dulles, *Models of Revelation*, 229.

43. "On entend communément par révélations privées celles dont un âme, chrétienne ou non, est l'objet de la part de Dieu à titre personnel et privé, et non au titre d'initiateur ou de docteur en la religion universelle au sein de laquelle Dieu opère le salut de l'humanité." See Yves Congar, "La crédibilité des révélations privées," 29, translation mine.

44. See Benedict XIV, *De servorum Dei*, 1.2, ch. 32, n11.

45. Staehlin, in *Apariciones* 40, n35, cites Benedict XIV's *De servorum Dei* in stating that even in the case of private revelations officially approved by the Church, like that of Blessed Hildegard, Saint Bridget, or Catherine of Siena, one need not believe with *fides catholica*, but rather with *fides humana*: *Quaeres quarto, quid dicendum sit de revelationibus privatis a Sede Apostolica approbatis, ex. Gr. Beatae Hildegardis, et Sanctarum Birgittae, et Catharinae Senensis. Porro* (1.2, ch. 32, n11) *diximus, praedictis revelationibus, etsi approbatis, non debere, nec posse a nobis adhiberi assensum Fidei catholicae, sed tantum fidei humanae, iuxta regulas prudentiae, iuxta quas praedictae revelationes sunt probabiles, et pie credibiles* (1.3, ch. 53, n15).

46. Congar, "La crédibilité des révélations privées," 29–43.

47. The Lourdes apparition is an instance of a private revelation that has repeatedly received papal approval. One wonders, however, whether this approval covers only the doctrinal content of the revelations or also the "objective reality of the phenomenon (vision, apparition, locution) through which the revelations take form and are communicated" (Adnès, "Revelations, Private," 953).

48. Among the minimalists are found Carlos María Staehlin, S.I. See his *Apariciones*. Among the maximalists are found Adnès, Rahner, Congar, and Hvidt. For a discussion of this issue, see Hvidt, *Christian Prophecy*, 271–276.

49. Benedict XIV, *De servorum Dei*, 2.32.11.

50. De Guibert, *Documenta ecclesiastica christianae perfectionis*, xi, 509, translation altered from "purely" to "merely."

51. Pius X, *Pascendi dominici gregis* no. 55. Translation altered. The Latin reads: *Ecclesiam tanta in hac re uti prudentia, ut traditiones eiusmodine scripto narrari permittat nisi cautione multa adhibita praemissaque declaratione ab Urbano VIII. sanctita; quod etsi rite fiat, non tamen facti veritatem asserit, sed, nisi humana ad credendum argumenta desint, credi modo non prohibet.* I thank Jeremy Wilkins for pointing me to this translation issue.

52. The official document remains unpublished. A French translation can be found in Bouflet and Boutry, *Un signe dans le ciel*, 396–399.

53. In 1966 the *Index* was formally abolished by Paul VI, bringing to a formal end centuries-long prohibition by ecclesiastical authorities. See Kingham, "The Norms for Judging Alleged Apparitions and Private Revelations," 151.

54. Poulain, *The Graces of Interior Prayer*, 323.

55. Groeschel, *A Still, Small Voice*, 27.

56. Msgr. Alfredo Ottaviani, in a widely distributed address, urged the exercise of extreme caution and prudence ("The Need for Prudence").

57. See Burrell, *Freedom and Creation in Three Traditions*. Some of this work is well underway. Mark Swanson, in "The Trinity in Christian-Muslim Conversation," argues that the Muslim doctrine of *shirk* (the sin of idolatry or polytheism) can help Christians purify their Trinitarian language. Jon Hoover considers Muslim criticisms of the Trinity and outlines structural similarities between Islamic and Christian doctrines of God. See his "Islamic Monotheism and the Trinity."

58. Madigan, "*Nostra Aetate* and the Questions It Chose to Leave Open," 787–788.

59. While there is certainly much more work to do, some Christians have recently begun to offer theological readings of the Qur'an. From a Reformed and Evangelical perspective, see Anderson, *The Qur'an in Context*. One can also find many sources in the publications that have emerged over the past fifteen years from the Building Bridges Seminar. The Berkeley Center for Religion, Peace, and World Affairs at Georgetown University has spearheaded this effort. For a list of publications, see https://berkleycenter.georgetown.edu. See also Reynolds, *The Qur'an and Its Biblical Subtext*, and *The Qur'an and the Bible*.

60. Ochs, "Faith in the Third Millennium," 1.

BIBLIOGRAPHY

Adnès, Pierre. "Revelations, Private." In *Dictionary of Fundamental Theology*, ed. René Latourelle. New York: Crossroad, 1994, 950–54. Originally published as "Révélations Privées." In *Dictionnaire de spiritualité: Ascétique et mystique, doctrine et histoire*, 17 vols., ed. Marcel Viller, S.J., assisted by F. Cavallera and J. de Guibert, S.J. Paris: Beauchesne, 1932–55.

Alberigo, Giuseppe, and Joseph A. Komonchak, eds. *History of Vatican II*. 5 vols. Maryknoll, NY: Orbis and Leuven Peeters, 1995–2006.

Alberigo, Giuseppe, Jean Pierre Jossua, Joseph A. Komonchak, and Matthew J. O'Connell. *The Reception of Vatican II*. Washington, DC: Catholic University of America Press, 1987.

Altmann, Alexander. "Maimonides and Thomas Aquinas: Natural or Divine Prophecy?" *Association for Jewish Studies Review* 3 (1978).

Anawati, Georges C., O.P. "An Assessment of the Christian-Islamic Dialogue." In *The Vatican, Islam, and the Middle East*, ed. Kail C. Ellis, O.S.A. Syracuse, NY: Syracuse University Press, 1987.

———. "Excursus on Islam." *In Commentary on the Documents of Vatican II*, ed. Herbert Vorgrimler, vol. 3. New York: Crossroad, 1989.

Anderson, Mark Robert. *The Qur'an in Context: A Christian Exploration*. Downers Grove, IL: Intervarsity Press, 2016.

Aquinas, Thomas. *Commentary on the First Epistle to the Corinthians*. Trans. Fabian Larcher, O.P. Lander, WY: Aquinas Institute for the Study of Sacred Doctrine, 2012. Originally published as *Commentary on the First Epistle to the Corinthians*. Trans. Fabian Larcher, O.P., and Daniel Keating. Albany: Magi, 1998.

———. *Commentary on the Letter of Saint Paul to the Hebrews*. Trans. Fabian Larcher, O.P. Available at https://dhspriory.org.

———. *Expositio super Isaiam ad litteram*, cura et studio Fratrum Praedicatorum. Rome: Editori di San Tommaso, 1974.

———. *In Ioannes (In Io.)*. Trans. Fabian R. Larcher, O.P. Albany: Magi Books, 1998.

———. *In Isaiam* (*In Is.*). In *Sancti Thomae de Aquino opera omnia*, iussu Leonis XIII. P. M. edita. Vol. 28: *Expositio super Isaiam ad litteram*, cura et studio Fratrum Praedicatorum. Rome: Typo. Polyglotta, 1989. Originally published in Rome: San Tommaso, 1974.

———. *Quaestiones Disputatae De Potentia Dei* 6.5 *ad.* 3. English translation: *On the Power of God*. Trans. English Dominican Fathers. Westminster, MD: Newman, 1932.

———. *Quaestiones Disputatae De Veritate* 12.3 *ad.* 1. English translation: *On Truth*. Trans. Robert W. Mulligan, S. J. Chicago: Henry Regnery, 1952.

———. *Summa contra gentiles* (*ScG*). Trans. Anton C. Pegis. New York: Hanover House, 1955–57.

———. *Summa theologiae*. Trans. Fathers of the English Dominican Province. New York: Benziger Brothers, 1947. Available at http://www.dhspriory .org/thomas/summa/.

———. *Super Hebraeos* (*Super Heb.*), *rep. vulgate*. In *St. Thomas Aquinas' Works in English*, trans. Fabian R. Larcher, O.P. Washington, DC: Dominican House of Studies, Priory of the Immaculate Conception. Available at http://www.dhspriory.org.

Arana, Andrés Ibáñez. "Las Cuestiones 'De Prophetia' en Santo Tomás y la Inspiración Bíblica." *Scriptorium Victoriense* 1, no. 2 (1954).

Augustine. *Tract. in Io*. Trans. John W. Rettig. Washington, DC: Catholic University of America Press, 1988.

Aydin, Mahmut. "Contemporary Christian Evaluations of the Prophet Muhammad." *Encounters: Journal of Intercultural Perspectives* 6, no. 1 (March 2000).

Barnes, Michael, S.J. "Opening Up a Dialogue: *Dei Verbum* and the Religions." *Modern Theology* 29, no. 4 (October 2013): 10–31.

Bauerschmidt, Frederick Christian. *Holy Teaching: Introducing the Summa Theologiae of Thomas Aquinas*. Grand Rapids, MI: Brazos, 2005.

Benedict XIV, Pope. *Benedicti papae XIV doctrina de servorum Dei beatificatione et beatorum canonizatione in synopsim redacta ab emm. de Azevedo*. Brussels: Typis Societatis Belgicae de Propagandis Bonis Libris, 1840.

———. *De Servorum Dei Beatificatione et Beatorum Canonizatione di Congregazione per le Cause dei Santi*. Vol. I.1. Libreria Editrice Vaticana.

Benedict XVI, Pope. "A Proper Hermeneutic for the Second Vatican Council." In *Vatican II: Renewal within Tradition*, ed. Matthew L. Lamb and Matthew Levering. Oxford: Oxford University Press, 2008.

———. "Meeting with Representatives of Some Muslim Communities," August 20, 2005. Available at http://w2.vatican.va/.

———. *Spe Salvi*. Encyclical, November 30, 2007. Available at http://w2 .vatican.va/.

———. "*Verbum domini*." Post-Synodal Apostolic Exhortation no. 14, September 30, 2010. Available at http://w2.vatican.va/.

Benoit, Pierre, O.P. "Révélation et inspiration selon la Bible, chez saint Thomas et dans les discussions modernes." *Revue Biblique* 70 (1963): 321–72.

Benoit, Pierre, O.P., and Pierre Synave. *Saint Thomas d'Aquin. Somme Théologique*, 2a2ae, questions 171–178, *La Prophétie*, 2a2ae, questions 171–178. Tournai: Éditions de la Revue des Juenes, 1947.

Boeve, Lieven. "Revelation, Scripture and Tradition: Lessons from Vatican II's Constitution *Dei verbum* for Contemporary Theology." *International Journal of Systematic Theology* 13, no. 4 (2011): 416–33.

Bouflet, Joachim, and Philippe Boutry. *Un signe dans le ciel*. Paris: Grasset, 1997.

Buckley, Michael J. *Denying and Disclosing God: The Ambiguous Progress of Modern Atheism*. New Haven, CT: Yale University Press, 2004.

Burrell, David, C.S.C. "Analogy, Creation, and Theological Language." *Proceedings of the American Catholic Philosophical Association* 74 (2000).

———. *Aquinas: God and Action*. Notre Dame, IN: University of Notre Dame Press, 1979.

———. "Argument in Theology: Analogy and Narrative." *Journal of the American Academy of Religion* 49, no. 1 (1982).

———. "Faith, Culture, and Reason: Analogous Language and Truth." *Proceedings of the American Catholic Philosophical Association* 77 (2003).

———. *Freedom and Creation in Three Traditions*. Notre Dame, IN: University of Notre Dame Press, 1993.

———. *Knowing the Unknowable God: Ibn-Sina, Maimonides, Aquinas*. Notre Dame, IN: University of Notre Dame Press, 1986.

Burtchaell, J. T. *Catholic Theories of Biblical Inspiration since 1810: A Review and Critique*. Cambridge: Cambridge University Press, 1969.

Casciaro, José María. *El diálogo de Santo Tomás con Musulmanes y Judíos: El Tema de la Profecía y de la Revelación*. Madrid: Imprenta Aguirre, 1968.

———. "Santo Tomás ante sus fuentes (estudio sobre la II–II q 173 a 3)." *Scripta theologica* 6, no. 1 (1974).

Caspar, R. "Le Concile et l'Islam." *Etudes* 324 (1966): 114–26.

———. "La religion musulamanne: Élaboration et commentarie de texte de la Déclaration." *Unum Sanctum* 61 (Paris, 1966).

Cassidy, Edward Idris Cardinal. *Ecumenism and Interreligious Dialogue: Unitatis Redintegratio, Nostra Aetate*. New York: Paulist Press, 2005.

Catechism of the Catholic Church. Washington, DC: United States Conference of Catholic Bishops, 1994.

Cavanaugh, William T. "Religious Violence as Modern Myth." *Political Theology* 15, no. 6 (November 2014): 486–502.

Clifford, Catherine E. *Decoding Vatican II: Interpretation and Ongoing Reception.* New York: Paulist Press, 2014.

Clooney, Francis, S.J. *Divine Mary, Blessed Mother: Hindu Goddesses and the Virgin Mary.* Oxford: Oxford University Press, 2005.

———. *Hindu God, Christian God: How Reason Helps Break Down the Boundaries between Religions.* Oxford: Oxford University Press, 2001.

———. "Implications for the Practice of Inter-religious Learning." In *Sic et Non: Encountering* Dominus Iesus, ed. Stephen J. Pope and Charles Hefling. New York: Orbis, 2002.

———. "Saving *Dominus Iesus.*" In *Learned Ignorance: Intellectual Humility among Jews, Christians, and Muslims*, ed. James L. Heft, S.M., Reuven Firestone, and Omid Safi. Oxford: Oxford University Press, 2011.

Cohen, Charles, Paul Knitter, and Ulrich Rosenhagen, eds. *The Future of Interreligious Dialogue: A Multi-Religious Conversation on* Nostra Aetate. Maryknoll, NY: Orbis, 2017.

Colberg, Shawn M. "Aquinas and the Grace of Auxilium." *Modern Theology* 32, no. 2 (2016).

Congar, Yves. "La crédibilité des révélations privées." *Vie spirituelle* 53 (1937): Supplément, 29–48.

Congregation for the Doctrine of the Faith. *Dominus Iesus: On the Unicity and Salvific Universality of Jesus Christ and the Church.* 2000. http://www.vatican.va/roman_curia/congregations/cfaith/documents/rc_con_cfaith_doc_20000806_dominus-iesus_en.html.

Cox, Harvey. *The Market as God.* Cambridge, MA: Harvard University Press, 2016.

Cragg, Kenneth. *The Call of the Minaret.* New York: Oxford University Press, 1956.

———. *Muhammad and the Christian.* Maryknoll, NY: Orbis, 1984.

———. *The Weight in the Word—Prophethood: Biblical and Quranic.* Brighton, England: Sussex Academic Press, 1999.

Dakake, Maria. "Theological Parallels and Metaphysical Meeting Points." In *Muslim and Christian Understanding: Theory and Application of "A Common Word,"* ed. Waleed El-Ansary and David K. Linnan. New York: Palgrave Macmillan, 2010.

Daniel, Norman. *Islam and the West: The Making of an Image.* Edinburgh: Edinburgh University Press, 1960.

Danish Medical Association (laeger.dk). "Lægeforeningen: Omskæring bør kun foretages efter informeret samtykke fra den unge mand selv." *Lægeforeningen*, December 2, 2016. Available at http://www.laeger.dk/.

Dauphinais, Michael. *Aquinas the Augustinian.* Washington, DC: Catholic University of America Press, 2007.

D'Costa, Gavin. *Vatican II: Catholic Doctrines on Jews and Muslims.* Oxford: Oxford University Press, 2014.

———, ed. "Whose Objectivity? Which Neutrality? The Doomed Quest for a Neutral Vantage Point from Which to Judge Religions." *Religious Studies* 29 (1993).

———. *Christian Uniqueness Reconsidered: Myth of Pluralistic Theology of Religions.* Maryknoll, NY: Orbis, 1990.

de Guibert, Joseph. *Documenta ecclesiastica christianae perfectionis: Studium spectantia* no. 1005. Rome: Gregorian University, 1931. Citing *Acta Sanctae Sedis* (Rome, 1865).

Denzinger, Heinrich. *Compendium of Creeds, Definitions, and Declarations on Matters of Faith and Morals* 43. Ed. Peter Hünermann, Robert Fastiggi, and Anne Englund Nash. San Francisco: Ignatius Press, 2010.

———. *The Sources of Catholic Dogma.* Trans. Roy J. Deferrari. St. Louis: Herder, 1957.

Dhavamony, Mariasusai, S.J. "Evangelization and Dialogue in Vatican II and in the 1974 Synod." In Mariasusai, *Vatican II: Assessment and Perspectives*, vol. 3, 264–81. New York: Paulist Press, 1989.

Dulles, Avery, S.J., *The Assurance of Things Hoped For: A Theology of Christian Faith.* New York: Oxford University Press, 1994.

———. *Models of Revelation.* Maryknoll, NY: Orbis, 1992.

Dupuis, Jacques, S.J. "Interreligious Dialogue in the Church's Evangelizing Mission: Twenty Years of Evolution of a Theological Concept." In Mariasusai, *Vatican II: Assessment and Perspectives; Twenty-Five Years After (1962–1987)*, ed. René Latourelle. 3 vols. New York: Paulist Press, 1989.

———. *Jesus Christ and His Spirit: Theological Approaches.* Bangalore: Theological Publications in India, 1977.

———. "A Theological Commentary: Dialogue and Proclamation." In *Redemption and Dialogue: Reading* Redemptoris Missio *and* Dialogue and Proclamation, ed. William R. Burrows. Maryknoll, NY: Orbis, 1994.

El-Ansary, Waleed, and David K. Linnan, eds. *Muslim and Christian Understanding: Theory and Application of "A Common Word."* New York: Palgrave Macmillan, 2010.

Elders, Leo. "Les rapports entre la doctrine de la prophétie de saint Thomas et 'le Guide des égarés de Maïmonide.'" *Divus Thomas* 78 (1975).

Emery, Giles. *The Trinitarian Theology of St. Thomas Aquinas*, trans. F. A. Murphy. Oxford: Oxford University Press, 2007.

Faggioli, Massimo. *Vatican II: The Battle for Meaning.* New York: Paulist Press, 2012.

Farkasfalvy, Denis, O. Cist. *Inspiration and Interpretation: A Theological Introduction to Sacred Scripture.* Washington, DC: Catholic University of America Press, 2010.

Farrugia, Joseph. *The Church and the Muslims: The Church's Consideration of Islam and the Muslims in the Documents of the Second Vatican Council.* Malta: Gozo, 1988.

Fesquet, Henri. *The Drama of Vatican II: The Ecumenical Council, June 1962– December 1965.* New York: Random House, 1967.

Fitzgerald, Michael Louis, M. Afr. " 'Dialogue and Proclamation': A Reading in the Perspective of Christian-Muslim Relations." In *Many and Diverse Ways: In Honor of Jacques Dupuis,* ed. Daniel Kendall and Gerald O'Collins. Maryknoll, NY: Orbis, 2003.

Ford, David F., and C. C. Pecknold, eds. *The Promise of Scriptural Reasoning.* Malden, MA: Wiley-Blackwell, 2006.

Fox, Jonathan. "Paradigm Lost: Huntington's Unfulfilled Clash of Civilizations Prediction into the 21st Century." *International Politics* 42 (2005): 428–57.

Fredericks, James. "The Catholic Church and the Other Religious Paths: Rejecting Nothing That Is True and Holy." *Theological Studies* 64 (2003).

GRIC (Groupe de Recherche Islamo-Chrétien). *The Challenge of the Scriptures: The Bible and the Qur'an.* Maryknoll, NY: Orbis, 1989. Original French edition: *Ces Écritures qui nous questionnent: La Bible et le Coran.* Paris: Le Centurion, 1987.

Groeschel, Benedict J. *A Still, Small Voice: A Practical Guide on Reported Revelations.* San Francisco: Ignatius, 1993.

Hart, David Bentley. *Atheist Delusions: The Christian Revolution and Its Fashionable Enemies.* New Haven, CT: Yale University Press, 2010.

Heft, James L., S. M., and John O'Malley. "Introduction: Trajectories and Hermeneutics." In *After Vatican II: Trajectories and Hermeneutics,* ed. Heft and O'Malley. Grand Rapids, MI: Eerdmans, 2012.

Hibbs, Thomas. *Dialectic and Narrative in Aquinas: An Interpretation of the Summa contra Gentiles.* Notre Dame, IN: University of Notre Dame Press, 1995.

Hick, John H., and Paul F. Knitter, eds. *The Myth of Christian Uniqueness: Towards a Pluralistic Theology of Religion.* Maryknoll, NY: Orbis, 1987.

The Holy Bible: The New Revised Standard Version, Catholic Edition. New York: Oxford University Press, 1999.

Hoover, Jon. "Islamic Monotheism and the Trinity." *Conrad Grebel Review* 27, no. 1 [Winter 2009]: 57–82.

Hünermann, Peter, and Bernd Jochen Hilberath, eds. *Herder theologischer Kommentar zum zweiten Vatikanischen Konzil.* Freiburg im Breisgau: Herder, 2004–6.

Huntington, Samuel. *The Clash of Civilizations and the Remaking of World Order.* New York: Simon and Schuster, 1996.

Hütter, Reinhard, and Matthew Levering. *Ressourcement Thomism: Sacred Doctrine, the Sacraments, and the Moral Life.* Washington, DC: Catholic University of America Press, 2010.

Hvidt, Christian Niels. *Christian Prophecy: The Post-Biblical Tradition.* Oxford: Oxford University Press, 2007.

Islamochristiana. Rome: Pontifical Institute for Arabic and Islamic Studies (PISAI) 44 (1978).

Jenkins, Philip. *God's Continent: Christianity, Islam and Europe's Religious Crisis.* Oxford: Oxford University Press, 2009.

———. *The New Faces of Christianity: Believing the Bible in the Global South.* Oxford: Oxford University Press, 2006.

John of Damascus. *Writings: The Fount of Knowledge—The Philosophical Chapters, On Heresies, the Orthodox Faith*, vol. 37. New York: The Fathers of the Church, 1958.

John Paul II, Pope. *DI 7.* In *Heinrich Denzinger Compendium of Creeds, Definitions, and Declarations on Matters of Faith and Morals*, 43. Ed. Peter Hünermann, Robert Fastiggi, and Anne Englund Nash. San Francisco: Ignatius Press, 2010.

———. *Ut unum sint* (On Commitment to Ecumenism), no. 80. Available at http://w2.vatican.va/.

Jomier, Jacques, O.P. *The Great Themes of the Qur'an.* Trans. Zoe Hersov. London: SCM Press, 1997.

———. *How to Understand Islam.* New York: Crossroad, 1989.

Kaplan, Grant. "Vatican II as a Constitutional Text of Faith." *Horizons* 41, no. 1 (June 2014): 1–21.

Kerr, David A. "He Walked in the Path of the Prophets: Toward a Christian Theological Recognition of the Prophethood of Muhammad." In *Christian-Muslim Encounters*, ed. Yvonne Yazbeck Haddad and Wadi Zaiden Haddad. Gainesville, FL: University Press of Florida, 1995.

———. "Muhammad: Prophet of Liberation—A Christian Perspective from Political Theology." *Studies in World Christianity* 6, no. 2 (February 2011).

———. "The Prophet Muhammad in Christian Theological Perspective." *International Bulletin of Missionary Research* 8, no. 3 (1984).

Khan, Abrahim. "Metatheological Reflections on Recent Christian Acknowledgement of Muhammad as Prophet: Inter-Faith Dialogue and the Academic Study of Religion." *Toronto Journal of Theology* 2, no. 2 (1986).

Khodr, George. "L'Arabité." In *Pentalogie Islamo-Chrétienne*, ed. Youkim Moubarac. Beirut: Éditions du Cenacle Libanais, 1972–73. Vol. 5: *Palestine et Arabité.*

Kingham, Andre. "The Norms for Judging Alleged Apparitions and Private Revelations." Ph.D. diss., St. Paul University, St. Paul, MN, 2007.

Klubertanz, George P., S.J. *St. Thomas Aquinas on Analogy: A Textual Analysis and Systematic Synthesis*. Chicago: Loyola University Press, 1960.

Knitter, Paul F., ed. *The Myth of Religious Superiority: Multifaith Explorations of Religious Pluralism*. New York: Orbis, 2005.

Körtner, U. H. J. *Der Inspüerte Leser: Zentrale Aspekte biblischer Hermeutik*. Gottingen: Vandenhoeck and Ruprecht, 1994.

Krokus, Christian. "Louis Massignon: Vatican II and Beyond." *Logos: A Journal of Eastern Christian Studies* 55, nos. 3–4 (2014): 433–50.

———. "Louis Massignon's Influence on the Teaching of Vatican II on Muslims and Islam." *Islam and Christian-Muslim Relations* 23, no. 3 (2012): 329–45.

———. *The Theology of Louis Massignon: Islam, Christ, and the Church*. Washington, DC: Catholic University of America Press, 2017.

Küng, Hans. "The Charismatic Structure of the Church." *Concilium* 4, no. 1 (1965): 23–33.

———. *Christianity and the World Religions*. Trans. P. Heinegg. London: Collins, 1985.

———. *Islam: Past, Present and Future*. Trans. John Bowden. Oxford: Oneworld, 2007. Original German edition: *Der Islam: Geschichte, Gegenwart, Zukunft*. Munich: Piper, 2004.

———. "Radical Changes in History—Challenges of the Present." In *Islam and Enlightenment: New Issues*, ed. Erik Borgman and Pim Valkenberg. London: SCM-Canterbury, 2005.

———. "Towards an Ecumenical Theology of Religions: Some Theses for Clarification." In *Christianity and World Religions*, ed. Hans Küng and Jürgen Moltmann. Edinburgh: T and T Clark, 1986.

Lamb, Matthew L., and Matthew Levering. *Vatican II: Renewal within Tradition*. Oxford: Oxford University Press, 2008.

Latourelle, René. *Theology of Revelation: Including a Commentary on the Constitution "Dei Verbum" of Vatican II*. Eugene, OR: Wipf and Stock, 2009.

Laurentin, René. *The Apparitions of the Blessed Virgin Mother Today*. Trans. Luke Griffin. Dublin: Veritas, 1990.

Lehner, Ulrich. *The Catholic Enlightenment: The Forgotten History of a Global Movement*. Oxford: Oxford University Press, 2016.

Levering, Matthew. *An Introduction to Vatican II as an Ongoing Theological Event*. Washington, DC: Catholic University of America Press, 2017.

———. *Christ's Fulfillment of Torah and Temple: Salvation According to Thomas Aquinas*. Notre Dame, IN: University of Notre Dame Press, 2002.

———. *Participatory Biblical Exegesis: A Theology of Biblical Interpretation*. Notre Dame, IN: University of Notre Dame Press, 2008.

———. *Scripture and Metaphysics: Aquinas and the Renewal of Trinitarian Theology.* Oxford: Wiley-Blackwell, 2004.

Lilla, Mark. "The Politics of God." *New York Times Magazine*, August 19, 2007. Available at http://query.nytimes.com/.

———. *The Stillborn God: Religion, Politics and the Modern West.* New York: Alfred A. Knopf, 2007.

———. "The Truth About [sic] Our Libertarian Age." *New Republic*, June 17, 2014. Available at http://www.newrepublic.com/.

Lumbard, Joseph. "What of the Word Is in Common?" In *Muslim and Christian Understanding: Theory and Application of "A Common Word,"* ed. Waleed El-Ansary and David K. Linnan. New York: Palgrave Macmillan, 2010.

Lyttkens, Hampus. *The Analogy between God and the World: An Investigation of Its Background and Interpretation of Its Use by Thomas of Aquino.* Uppsala, Sweden: Almqvist and Wiksells, 1952.

MacIntyre, Alasdair. *Whose Justice? Which Rationality?* Notre Dame, IN: University of Notre Dame Press, 1989.

Madigan, Daniel A., S.J. "Jesus and Muhammad: The Sufficiency of Prophecy." In *Bearing the Word: Prophecy in Biblical Qur'anic Perspective*, ed. Michael Ipgrave. London: Church House, 2005.

———. "Mary and Muhammad: Bearers of the Word." *Australasian Catholic Record* 80, no. 4 (2003): 417–27.

———. "Mutual Theological Hospitality: Doing Theology in the Presence of the 'Other.'" In *Muslim and Christian Understanding: Theory and Application of "A Common Word,"* ed. Waleed El-Ansary and David K. Linnan. New York: Palgrave Macmillan, 2010.

———. "*Nostra Aetate* and the Questions It Chose to Leave Open." *Gregorianum* 87 (2006): 781–96.

———. "Saving *Dominus Iesus.*" In *Learned Ignorance: Intellectual Humility among Jews, Christians, and Muslims*, ed. James L. Heft, S. M., Reuven Firestone, and Omid Safi. Oxford: Oxford University Press, 2011.

Magno, Alberto. *Quaestio de prophetia: Visione, immaginazione e dono profetico.* Ed. Anna Rodolfi. Florence: Edizioni del Galluzzo, 2009.

Mahbubani, Kishore, and Lawrence Summers. "The Fusion of Civilizations: The Case for Global Optimism." *Foreign Affairs* 95, no. 3 (2016). Available at https://www.foreignaffairs.com/.

Manent, Pierre. *Beyond Radical Secularism: How France and the Christian West Should Respond to the Islamic Challenge.* Chicago, IL: Saint Augustine's Press, 2016.

Marchetto, Agostino. *The Second Vatican Ecumenical Council: A Counterpoint for the History of the Council.* Trans. Kenneth D. Whitehead. Scranton, PA: University of Scranton Press, 2010.

Martin, Francis. "Revelation and Its Transmission." In *Vatican II: Renewal within Tradition*, ed. Matthew L. Lamb and Matthew Levering. Oxford: Oxford University Press, 2008.

Mattison, William. *Introducing Moral Theology: True Happiness and the Virtues*. Grand Rapids, MI: Brazos, 2008.

McCarthy, Brian. "El modo del conocimiento profético y escriturístico en Santo Tomás de Aquino." *Scripta Theologica* 9, no. 2 (1977).

McGinn, Bernard. "Prophetic Power in Early Medieval Christianity." *Cristianesimo nella storia* 17 (1996): 251–69.

McInerny, Ralph M. *Aquinas and Analogy*. Washington, DC: Catholic University of America Press, 1996.

———. *The Logic of Analogy: An Interpretation of St. Thomas*. The Hague: Nijhoff, 1961.

Michel, Thomas F. *A Muslim Theologian's Response to Christianity: Ibn Taymiyya's Al-Jawab Al-sahih in Contra Legem Saracenorum*. Delmar, NY: Caravan, 1984.

Miller, John. *Vatican II: An Interfaith Appraisal*. Notre Dame, IN: University of Notre Dame Press, 1966.

Montag, John. "Revelation: The False Legacy of Suarez." In *Radical Orthodoxy: A New Theology; Suspending the Material*, ed. John Milbank, Catherine Pickstock, and Graham Ward. London: Routledge, 1998.

Montagnes, Bernard, O.P. *La Doctrine de l'analogie de l'être d'après Saint Thomas d'Aquin*. Louvain, Belgium: Publications Universitaires, 1963.

Moreland, Anna Bonta. "An Analogical Reading of Christian Prophecy: The Case of Muhammad." *Modern Theology* 29, no. 4 (October 2013).

———. *Known by Nature: Thomas Aquinas on Natural Knowledge of God*. New York: Crossroad, 2010.

———. "The Qur'an and the Doctrine of Private Revelation: A Theological Proposal." *Theological Studies* 76, no. 3 (2015): 531–49.

Muslim-Christian Research Group. *The Challenge of the Scriptures: The Bible and the Qur'ān*. Trans. Stuart E. Brown. Maryknoll, NY: Orbis, 1989.

Nader, Albert. "L'Influence de la pensée musulmane sur la philosophie de Saint Thomas d'Aquin." In *Il Pensiero di Tomaso d'Aquino: E il Problemi Fondamentali del Nostro Tempo*. Roma: Herder, 1974.

New American Bible. New York: Oxford University Press, 1990.

Ochs, Peter. "Faith in the Third Millennium: Reading Scriptures Together." Address at the inauguration of Dr. Ian Torrance as president of Princeton Theological Seminary and professor of Patristics, Thursday, March 10, 2005. Available at http://jsrforum.lib.virginia.edu/ochs-princeton.pdf.

O'Collins, Gerald, S.J. *Rethinking Fundamental Theology: Toward a New Fundamental Theology*. New York: Oxford University, 2011.

———. *The Second Vatican Council on Other Religions*. Oxford: Oxford University, 2013.

O'Malley, John. "Introduction: Trajectories and Hermeneutics." In *After Vatican II: Trajectories and Hermeneutics*, ed. James L. Heft, S. M. Grand Rapids, MI: Eerdmans, 2012.

———. *What Happened at Vatican II?* Cambridge, MA: Belknap Press of Harvard University Press, 2008.

Osterreicher, John M. *Commentary on the Documents of Vatican II*, ed. Herbert Vorgimler. 5 vols. New York: Herder and Herder, 1969.

———. "Declaration on the Relationship of the Church to Non-Christian Religions: Introduction and Commentary," ed. Herbert Vorgimler. In *Commentary on the Documents of Vatican II*, vol. 3. New York: Herder and Herder, 1969.

Ottavianni, Msgr. Alfredo. "The Need for Prudence." *American Ecclesiastical Review* 124 [1951]: 321–26.

Paul VI, Pope. "*Lumen Gentium*: Dogmatic Constitution on the Church," November 21, 1964. Available at http://www.vatican.va/.

———. *Nostra Aetate: Declaration on the Revelation of the Church to Non-Christian Religions*, October 28, 1965, available at www.vatican.va/.

Pérez, Gonzalo Aranda. "Acerca de la verdad contenida en la Sagrada Escritura (una 'quaestio' de Santo Tomás citada por la Constitución 'Dei Verbum')." *Scripta theologica* 9, no. 2 (1977).

Philpott, Daniel. *Just and Unjust Peace: An Ethic of Political Reconciliation*. Oxford: Oxford University Press, 2012.

———. "Political Theology and Liberal Democracy." In *The Immanent Frame: Secularism, Religion and the Public Square*, January 23, 2008. New York: Social Science Research Council. Available at https://tif.ssrc.org/.

Pius X, Pope. *Pascendi dominici gregis* no. 55. Available at http://www.vatican.va/.

Pontifical Council for Interreligious Dialogue. *Dialogue and Proclamation* (May 19, 1991). Available at http://www.vatican.va/.

———. *Guidelines for Dialogue between Christians and Muslims*. Prepared by Maurice Borrmans. Trans. R. Marston Speight. New York: Paulist Press, 1981.

———. *Interreligious Dialogue: The Official Teaching of the Catholic Church from the Second Vatican Council to John Paul II (1963–2005)*, no. 16, ed. Francesco Gioia. Boston: Pauline, 2006.

Pontificio Istituto di Studi Arabi e d'Islamistica. "General Guidelines for True Dialogue: Basic Charter of GRIC, Muslim-Christian Research Group." *Islamochristiana* 4 (1978): 9–14, 175–186. Original French edition: *Ces Écritures qui nous questionnent: La Bible et le Coran*. Paris: Le Centurion, 1987.

Pope, Stephen J., and Charles Hefling, ed. *Sic et Non: Encountering* Dominus Iesus. New York: Orbis, 2002.

Poulain, Augustin, S.J. *The Graces of Interior Prayer: A Treatise on Mystical Theology.* Trans. Leonora L. Yorke Smith. St. Louis: Herder and Herder, 1910.

The Qur'ān: A New Annotated Translation. Trans. A. J. Droge. Sheffield, England: Equinox, 2013.

Rahner, Karl. "Death of Jesus and the Closure of Revelation." *Theological Investigations* 18. Trans. Edward Quinn. Baltimore: Helicon, 1961, 132–42.

———. "Revelation." In *Encyclopedia of Theology: The Concise Sacramentum Mundi* (1975): 1453–73.

———. *Visions and Prophecies.* Trans. Charles Henkey and Richard Strachan. New York: Herder and Herder, 1963.

Reynolds, Gabriel Said. *The Qur'an and Its Biblical Subtext.* New York: Routledge, 2010.

———. *The Qur'an and the Bible: Text and Commentary.* New Haven, CT: Yale University Press, 2018.

Rogers, Paul Martin. "Thomas Aquinas and Prophecy: Divine Revelation and Its Interaction with Human Knowing." Ph.D. diss., University of Cambridge, 2014.

Ruokanen, Mikka. *The Catholic Doctrine of Non-Christian Religions according to the Second Vatican Council.* New York: E. J. Brill, 1992. Originally published in Leiden by Brill, 1982.

Rush, Ormond. *Still Interpreting Vatican II: Some Hermeneutical Principles.* Mahwah, NJ: Paulist Press, 2004.

———. "Toward a Comprehensive Interpretation of the Council and Its Documents." *Theological Studies* 73 (2012).

Said, Edward. "The Clash of Ignorance." *The Nation*, October 4, 2001. Available at https://www.thenation.com/.

Scatena, Silvia. *Vatican II.* London: SCM, 2012.

Schelkens, Karim. *Catholic Theology of Revelation on the Eve of Vatican II: A Redaction History of the Schema* De fontibus revelationis *(1960–1962).* Leiden: Brill, 2010.

Schultenover, David G., ed. *Vatican II: Did Anything Happen?* New York: Continuum International, 2007.

Schutz, Roger, and Fr. Max Thurian. *La parole vivante au Concile.* Taize, France: Presses de Taize, 1966.

Sen, Amartya. *Identity and Violence: The Illusion of Destiny.* New York: W. W. Norton, 2006.

Shah, Timothy S., and Allen D. Hertzke, eds. *Christianity and Freedom.* 6 vols. Cambridge: Cambridge University Press, 2016.

Siddiqui, Ataullah. *Christian-Muslim Dialogue in the Twentieth Century.* London: Macmillan, 1997.

Smith, Christian. *Religion: What It Is, How It Works and Why It Matters.* Princeton, NJ: Princeton University Press, 2017.

Southern, R. W. *Western Views of Islam in the Middle Ages.* Cambridge, MA: Harvard University Press, 1962.

Staehlin, Carlos María, S. I. *Apariciones: Ensayo crítico.* Madrid: "Razon y fe," 1954.

Suh, Augustinus. *Le rivelazioni private nella vita della Chiesa.* Bologna: Dehoniane, 2000.

Sullivan, Francis A., S.J. "Introduction and Ecclesiological Issues." In *Sic et non: Encountering* Dominus Iesus, ed. Stephen Pope and Charles Hefling. Maryknoll, NY: Orbis, 2002.

———. "Vatican II on the Salvation of the Adherents of Other Religions." In *After Vatican II: Trajectories and Hermeneutics*, ed. James Heft and John O'Malley. New York: Eerdmans, 2012.

Swanson, Mark N. "The Trinity in Christian-Muslim Conversation." *Dialog* 44 (2005): 256–63.

Tanner, Norman, ed. *Decrees of the Ecumenical Councils.* London: Sheed and Ward, 1990.

Tapie, Matthew. *Aquinas on Israel and the Church: The Question of Supersessionism in the Theology of Thomas Aquinas.* Eugene, OR: Wipf and Stock, 2014.

Thatamanil, John. "Learning From (and Not Just About) Our Religious Neighbors: Comparative Theology and the Future of *Nostra Aetate*." In *The Future of Interreligious Dialogue: A Multi-religious Conversation on* Nostra Aetate, edited by Charles L. Cohen, Paul F. Knitter, and Ulrich Rosenhagen. New York: Orbis, 2017.

Theobald, Christoph. "The Theological Option of Vatican II: Seeking an 'Internal' Principle of Interpretation." In *Vatican II: A Forgotten Future*, ed. Alberto Melloni and Christoph Theobald, 87–107. London: SCM Press, 2005.

Toft, Monica D., Daniel Philpott, and Samuel Shah. *God's Century: Resurgent Religion and Global Politics.* New York: W.W. Norton, 2011.

Tolan, John. *Saracens: Islam in the Medieval European Imagination.* New York: Columbia University Press, 2002.

———. *Mahomet l'Européen: Histoire des représentations du prophète en Occident.* Paris: Albin Michel, 2018.

Torrell, Jean-Pierre, O.P. "Les Charismes au service de la révélation," dans Thomas d'Aquin, *ST*, t. 3. Paris: Cerf, 1985.

———. *Saint Thomas Aquinas.* Vol. 1: *The Person and His Work.* Trans. Robert Royal. Washington, DC: Catholic University of America Press, 1996.

———. *Théorie de la prophétie et philosophie de la connaissance aux environs de 1230*. Louvain, Belgium: Spicilegium Sacrum Lovaniense, 1977.

———. *Thomas d'Aquin, Somme théologique, La Prophétie, 2a–2ae, Questions 171–178*, 2nd ed. Trans. P. Synave and P. Benoit. Paris: Cerf, 2005.

Toynbee, Arnold. *The World and the West*. Oxford: Oxford University Press, 1953.

Troll, Christian, S.J. "Catholicism and Islam." In *The Catholic Church and the World Religions: A Theological and Phenomenological Account*, ed. Gavin D'Costa. New York: T and T Clark, 2011.

———. *Dialogue and Difference: Clarity in Christian-Muslim Relations*. Maryknoll, NY: Orbis, 2009.

———. *Muslims Ask, Christians Answer*. German edition 2003. English translation Hyde Park, NY: New City Press, 2012.

Unsworth, Andrew. "A Historical and Textual-Critical Analysis of the Magisterial Documents of the Catholic Church on Islam: Towards a Heterodescriptive Account of Muslim Belief and Practice." Ph.D. diss., Heythrop College, London, 2007.

Valkenberg, Pim. *Sharing Lights on the Way to God: Muslim-Christian Dialogue and Theology in the Context of Abrahamic Partnership*. Amsterdam: Rodopi, 2006.

Vanhoye, Albert. "The Reception in the Church of the Dogmatic Constitution 'Dei Verbum.'" In *Opening Up the Scriptures: Joseph Ratzinger and the Foundations of Biblical Interpretation*, eds. Jose Granados, Carlos Granados, and Luis Sanchez-Navarro. Grand Rapids, MI: Eerdmans, 2008.

Vatican Council II. *Acta synodalia sacrosancti concilii oecumenici Vaticani II*, 5 vols. Vatican City: Typis Polyglottis Vaticanis, 1970–78.

———. *Ad gentes: On the Mission Activity of the Church*. Nairobi: Paulines, 2018.

———. *The Conciliar and Postconciliar Documents*. Trans. Austin Flannery. Northpoint, NY: Costello, 1996.

———. *Dei verbum*: "De divina revelatione: The Dogmatic Constitution on Divine Revelation of Vatican Council II." In *Decrees of the Ecumenical Councils*, ed. Norman Tanner. London: Sheed and Ward, 1990.

———. *Lumen Gentium*: "De ecclesia: The Dogmatic Constitution on the Church." In *Decrees of the Ecumenical Councils*, 16, ed. Norman Tanner. London: Sheed and Ward, 1990.

———. *Nostra Aetate*: "De habit. ad relig. non-Christianas: The Declaration on the Church's Relation to Non-Christian Religions," 3. In *Decrees of the Ecumenical Councils*, ed. Norman Tanner. London: Sheed and Ward, 1990.

Volken, Lauren. *Visions, Revelations, and the Church*. Trans. Edward Gallagher. New York: P. J. Kenedy, 1963.

Vorgrimler, Herbert, ed. *Commentary on the Documents of Vatican II.* 5 vols. New York: Herder and Herder, 1969.

Ward, Keith. "Muhammad from a Christian Perspective." In *Abraham's Children: Jews, Christians and Muslims in Conversation*, ed. Norman Solomon, Richard Harries, and Tim Winter. London: T and T Clark, 2005.

Watt, W. Montgomery. *Islam and Christianity Today.* New York: Routledge, 1983.

———. *Muhammad: Prophet and Statesman.* London: Oxford University Press, 1961.

———. *Muslim-Christian Encounters: Perceptions and Misperceptions.* New York: Routledge, 1991.

Wawrykow, Joseph P. *God's Grace and Human Action: "Merit" in the Theology of Thomas Aquinas.* Notre Dame, IN: University of Notre Dame Press, 1995.

Wenger, Antoine. *Vatican II.* Westminster, MD: Newman, 1966.

Wicks, Jared. "Vatican II on Revelation: From Behind the Scenes." *Theological Studies*, 71 (2010): 637–50.

Wilkins, Jeremy. "Love and Knowledge of God in the Human Life of Christ." *Pro Ecclesia* 21. no. 1 (Winter 2012): 77–99.

Williams, Rowan. *On Christian Theology.* Oxford: Wiley Blackwell, 2000.

Winter, Tim. "Jesus and Muhammad: New Convergences." *Muslim World* 99, no. 1 (2009): 21–38.

Wright, N. T. "How Can the Bible Be Authoritative?" *Vox Evangelica* (1991).

Zarb, S. M. "Le fonti agostiniane del trattato sulla profezia di S. Tommaso d'Aquino." *Angelicum* 15 (1938).

Zerafa, P. P. "The Limits of Biblical Inerrancy." *Angelicum* 39 (1962): 92–119.

INDEX

Abraham, 12, 22, 27–28, 31, 103
Ad gentes, 36
Agabus, 14, 55, 59
analogy, 116–20. *See also* Aquinas,
    Thomas
Anawati, Georges, O. P., 7, 136n30
Aquinas, Thomas
    and analogy, 116–20
    and Balaam, 8, 66, 72, 78–80, 82,
        85
    and Balaam's donkey, 76–77
    and Caiaphas, 66–75
    and Muhammad, 44–45
    and prophecy, 43–86
    and *revelatio*, 13
    and Roman soldiers, 75–76
    and *sacra doctrina*, 47–48, 52, 54
    and Solomon, 79–80
    and Vatican II, 13
āyāt, 99

Balaam, 8, 66, 72, 78–80, 82, 85
Balaam's donkey, 76–77
Barnes, Michael, S. J., 33
Benedict XVI, 11, 23, 33–34, 37,
    122
Borrmans, Maurice, M. Afr., 35
Buckley, Michael, 2–3
Burrell, David, C. S. C., 117–21,
    131

Caiaphas, 66–75, 82–83, 85
Caspar, Robert, M. Afr., 28, 31,
    136n30
Catholic Church
    *Catechism of the Catholic
        Church*, 122
    as mediator, 6
    prophetic dimension of, 34
    and salvation history, 34
    as sign of salvation, 27
Cavanaugh, William, 4–5
Christian revelation
    appropriation of, 25
    and closing of the canon, 28, 33
    cognitive aspects of, 21–22, 127
    dynamic model of, 26
    postbiblical, 17–18, 40, 124,
        126–28
    as public manifestation, 24
    verbal, 21
Clooney, Francis, S. J., 39
Commentary on Corinthians, 54,
    73–74, 78, 80
Commentary on Hebrews, 72–73,
    75, 79
Commentary on Isaiah, 58–59,
    147n60
Commentary on the Gospel of John,
    66–72
comparative theology, 10, 117

ANNA BONTA MORELAND

is associate professor of theology at Villanova University.
She is the author of *Known by Nature:*
Thomas Aquinas on Knowledge of God.

CPSIA information can be obtained
at www.ICGtesting.com
Printed in the USA
LVHW111304090320
649414LV00005B/42

9 780268 107253